THE COVID-19 PANDEMIC GREAT RESET

KLAUS JONES

Contents

INTRODUCTION 3

    Macro Reset First 12

    Interdependence....................................13

    Velocity 16

    Complexity 21

    Employment..22

What Future Growth Could Look Like...........................26

    Fiscal and Monetary Policies....................32

Which Is Worse, Inflation or Deflation?.....................35

What Will Happen To The USA Dollar? 36

    Resetting Society....................................40

    Inequalities...43

    Social Unrest 48

The Reemergence of "Large" Government...................53

    The Social Contract 60

    Reset of Geopolitics 68

    Nationalism and Globalization 71

    World Government 79

The Environment and The Coronavirus 84

    Air Pollution and Pandemic Risk 86

    Lockdown and Carbon Emissions............88

MICRO RESET (INDUSTRY AND BUSINESS)....................93

    CONCLUSION..97

INTRODUCTION

There has never been a crisis like the one the coronavirus epidemic has caused on a global scale. When we say that it is thrusting our world as a whole and each of us individually into the most difficult circumstances we've encountered in decades, we cannot be accused of exaggerating. It is a pivotal time in our history, and many things will never be the same as a result. Massive economic disruption is being brought about by it, and it is also making the political, social, and geopolitical climate unsafe and unstable. It is also widening the reach of technology in our lives, whether that is beneficial or harmful. The effects of these shifts will be seen across all businesses and industries. Many industries have an uncertain future and millions of businesses threaten extinction; only a select few will succeed. Numerous people report that their personal lives are disintegrating at an alarming rate. Deep existential crises, however, also encourage reflection and have the capacity to bring about change. People believe that the time for innovation has come as the world's fault lines, most notably social differences, unfairness, lack of cooperation, and failure of global governance and leadership, lie exposed as never before. There will be an entirely new world that we must both envision and sketch.

The pandemic is still getting worse across the globe as of this writing (June 2020). We all wonder when things will get back to normal. Never is the short answer. Because the coronavirus pandemic represents a crucial turning point in our global trajectory, nothing will ever return to the "broken" feeling of normalcy that predated the crisis. The world as we know it in the early months of 2020 is no longer there due to the epidemic, which some analysts refer to as a significant bifurcation and others as a severe crisis of "biblical" proportions. There will soon be radical changes of such magnitude that some pundits will use the terms "before the coronavirus" (BC) and "after the coronavirus" (AC) eras. The speed and unexpectedness of these changes will continue to astound us; as they interact with one another, they will have second-, third-, fourth-, and more order implications; cascading effects; and unexpected results. They will so create a "new normal" that is utterly apart from the one we will be gradually leaving behind. In the process, many of our preconceptions and opinions about how the world could or ought to look will be disproved.

However, extreme declarations (such "everything will change") and a binary, all-or-nothing approach to thinking should be used with extreme caution. Real life will, of course, be considerably more complicated. The pandemic may not entirely change the world on its own, but it is likely to hasten many of the changes that were already underway before it broke out, which will in turn trigger more changes. There is only one thing for certain: there won't be any linear changes and lots of abrupt discontinuities. The goal of COVID-19: The Great Reset is to highlight the changes that are coming, to shine light on them, and to offer some suggestions for how they can take on a more preferable and sustainable form.

To put things in perspective, let's note that viruses have been there for at least 300 million years, while the oldest bacteria have been alive for billions of years. This implies that pandemics have most certainly always existed and been a significant aspect of human history ever since people began traveling; for the last 2000 years, they have been the norm rather than the exception. Epidemics have historically shown to be a force for long-lasting and frequently radical change due to their innate disruptiveness: they have sparked riots, caused population clashes and military defeats, but they have also sparked innovations, redrawn national borders, and frequently paved the way for revolutions. The Byzantine Empire was forced to modify its direction after being hit by the Plague of Justinian in 541–542, and some civilizations even vanished altogether when the Aztec and Inca emperors perished along with the majority of their people due to European diseases. Additionally, imposing measures to try and contain them have always been a tool in the policy toolbox. Therefore, the seclusion and lockdowns enforced on a large portion of the planet to control COVID-19 are nothing new. They have long been a standard practice. The first instances of confinement were quarantines, which were implemented in an effort to stop the Black Death between 1347 and 1350. And around one-third of all Europeans perished in 1351. The idea of detaining people for 40 days originated from the word quaranta, which in Italian means "forty," without the authorities really understanding what they were trying to detain. Nevertheless, the measures were among the first examples of "institutionalized public health" and helped to justify the modern state's "accretion of power." The 40-day period was chosen for symbolic and religious reasons rather than for any medical justification. Both the Old and New Testaments frequently make reference to the number 40 in the context of purification, particularly the 40 days of Lent and the 40 days of the Genesis deluge.

The spread of infectious diseases has a special capacity for causing anxiety, fear, and widespread hysteria. As we've seen, doing so puts our social cohesiveness and capacity to manage a crisis at jeopardy. By their very nature, epidemics cause division and trauma. What we are fighting against is invisible; our loved ones, neighbors, and even our favorite daily rituals, like meeting a friend in public, could all become sources of infection; the authorities, who strive to keep us safe by implementing containment measures, are frequently seen as oppressive agents. The crucial and consistent trend throughout history has been to look for scapegoats and cast the blame squarely on the outsider. Jews were virtually invariably included in the victims of the most infamous pogroms caused by the plague in medieval Europe. This is best demonstrated by a terrible example: on Valentine's Day in 1349, two years after the Black Death began to ravage the continent, Jews in Strasbourg were ordered to convert after they were charged with contaminating the city's wells and spreading the disease. 1,000 people were burnt alive for refusing. Jews were forced to move in large numbers to eastern Europe

(Poland and Russia) during that same year after their communities in other European cities were wiped out, irreversibly changing the continent's demographics. What is true for European anti-Semitism also holds true for the growth of the absolutist state, the church's slow decline, and a host of other historical occurrences that are in large part due to pandemics. Feudalism and serfdom were abolished, and the age of enlightenment was inaugurated as a result of the reforms, which were so numerous and extensive that they marked "the end of an age of subjection." The Black Death may have been the unacknowledged start of modern man, to put it simply. If the plague could cause such significant social, political, and economic changes in the middle Ages, may the COVID-19 pandemic signal the beginning of a similar turning point with long-lasting and dramatic effects for our world today? Contrary to several earlier epidemics, COVID-19 doesn't provide a fresh existential danger. It won't lead to unanticipated major famines, significant military setbacks, or significant regime transitions. The pandemic won't wipe out entire populations or force them to relocate. This, however, does not constitute a comforting analysis. In essence, the epidemic is drastically escalating risks that already existed but that we have neglected to appropriately address for too long. Additionally, it will hasten troubling patterns that have been developing over a long period of time.

We require a conceptual framework (or a straightforward mental map) to aid in reflection and serve as a road map for understanding in order to start developing a meaningful answer. Historical perspectives can be especially useful. This is why, when faced with difficult issues about what will change and how much it will change, we frequently look for a comforting "mental anchor" that may act as a reference point. We do this by searching for examples and asking queries like: Is the pandemic comparable to the Spanish flu of 1918, which is thought to have killed over 50 million people in three waves throughout the world? Could it resemble the 1929–1933 Great Depression? Is there a similarity to the psychological trauma brought on by 9/11? Despite occurring on a different scale, are there parallels between what transpired with SARS in 2003 and H1N1 in 2009? Could it be much worse than the severe financial catastrophe of 2008? No is the appropriate answer to all of these, despite being undesired. None matches the scope and pattern of the current pandemic's economic devastation and human misery. Particularly, the economic aftermath differs significantly from any other catastrophe in recent memory. We are at war, but with an invisible adversary, as several heads of state and government have noted during the pandemic: "If what we are going through can actually be termed a war, it is surely not a traditional one. After all, humanity as a whole shares the adversary of today.

Despite this, it's still possible that one of the most useful mental anchors for determining what will happen next is World War II. The world order and the global economy underwent profound transformations as a result of World War II, which also resulted in significant social and economic developments.

Views and convictions that finally helped to establish revolutionary new laws and social contract clauses (like women joining the workforce before becoming voters). Although a pandemic and a war have clear fundamental differences (which we shall go into more depth about in the pages that follow), their levels of transformative power are comparable. Both could result in a crisis of transformation of hitherto unthinkable magnitude. But we must avoid using flimsy comparisons. COVID-19 will kill significantly fewer people than the Great Plagues, including the Black Deaths, or World War II, even in the most horrifying worst-case scenario. Additionally, the economies of the past centuries, which were based on manual labor, farms, and heavy industry, have little in common with those of the present. The consequences of the pandemic, however, will go much beyond the (already alarming) figures relating to death, unemployment, and bankruptcies in today's highly interconnected and interdependent world.

The writing and publication of COVID-19: The Great Reset take place in the midst of a crisis whose effects will be felt for many years to come. It is no surprise that we all feel a little perplexed since, when a major shock occurs, it brings with it the unsettling certainty that its results will be both unexpected and odd. Yet all these changes were, in a way, so extraordinary and had been made so hastily that it wasn't easy to see them as likely to have any permanency, as Albert Camus succinctly put it in his 1947 novel The Plague. What will occur in the immediate aftermath of the pandemic and then in the near future now that the unthinkable has already occurred?

Of fact, it is still far too early to predict with any degree of certainty what "momentous" changes COVID-19 will involve, but this book's goal is to provide as many clear and philosophically sound guidance as it can about what might lie ahead. Our goal is to aid readers in understanding the complex nature of the impending changes. At the very least, we will argue that the pandemic will hasten systemic changes that were already discernible before the crisis: the partial retreat from globalization, the growing decoupling between the US and China, the acceleration of automation, worries about increased surveillance, the growing appeal of well-being policies, rising nationalism and the ensuing fear of immigration, the growing power of tech, the requirement for firms to have an even stronger online presence. However, it might be able to transform things that had previously been immutable, going beyond merely accelerating. Thus, it might lead to adjustments that before the pandemic struck would have seemed unthinkable, such as new types of monetary policy like helicopter money (which is already a given), a reevaluation/recalibration of some of our social priorities and a heightened pursuit of the common good as a policy objective, the idea of fairness gaining political clout, radical welfare and taxation reforms, and drastic geopolitical realignments.

The larger point is that, for better or worse, the possibilities for change and the new order that results are now only limited by human imagination. Societies may be on the verge of becoming more egalitarian or authoritarian, or geared toward greater solidarity or individualism, favoring the interests of the few or the many. When economies recover, they may choose to move in the direction of greater inclusivity and be more sensitive to the needs of our global commons, or they may resume their previous patterns of operation. You get the idea: in order to make our planet a better and more robust one when it emerges from this catastrophe, we should make the most of this once-in-a-lifetime opportunity to rethink it.

We recognize that it would be a monumental task— possibly even impossible—to attempt to explore the range and depth of all the topics covered in this book. The topic and all the unknowns around it are enormous, and they could have covered five times as many pages as this publication. However, our goal was to develop a book that was quite brief and easy to read in order to aid the reader in understanding what is to come in a variety of fields. The reference material is near the conclusion of the book, and direct attributions have been kept to a minimum to minimize disruptions to the text's flow. It will constantly change to take into account the changing nature of the subject matter and be published in the thick of the crisis and when additional waves of infection are anticipated. Future iterations will be updated in light of fresh research, current policy directives, and continued reader feedback.

This book is a cross between an essay and a casual academic book. Both theory and application are covered.

There are various speculations and thoughts about what the post-pandemic world might, and perhaps should, look like, but it is primarily explanatory. We believe it will be helpful even though it doesn't provide any straightforward generalizations or suggestions for a world transitioning to a new normal.

This book's three main chapters, which provide a broad picture of the foreseeable future, are organized around. The first predicts the pandemic's effects on five important macro categories: the economy, society, geopolitics, environment, and technology. The second analyzes the impacts on certain businesses and industries in more detail. The third makes an assumption regarding the type of potential effects on a personal level.

Macro Reset First

The first leg of our journey moves through five macro categories that provide a thorough analytical framework to comprehend what is happening in the world today and how this may change in the future. We go through each separately, topically, for the sake of reading convenience. Our brains force us to think in linear terms, but the world around us is non-linear, which is to say: complicated, adaptive, fast-paced, and ambiguous. In actuality, they are interdependent, and this is where we start.

Conceptual framework: Three aspects that make up today's world.

The macro reset will take place in the context of the three dominant secular forces—interdependence, velocity, and complexity—that are currently shaping our world. We are all affected by this triumvirate, in varying degrees, regardless of who or where we are.

Interdependence

The word "interdependence" would have to be used to sum up the 21st century if only one word could. It is a by-product of globalization and technological advancement, and its basic definition is the dynamic of reciprocal dependency among the system's constituent parts. Some pundits claim that the globe is now "hyper connected" - a variation of interdependence on steroids - since globalization and technological development have grown so rapidly over the past several decades! What actually does this interdependence mean? Simply put, the entire globe is connected or "concatenated." A Singaporean researcher and former diplomat named Kishore Mahbubani described this situation in the early 2010s using the metaphor of a boat: "The 7 billion people who inhabit planet earth no longer reside in more than one hundred independent boats [countries]." Instead, they all share a single boat with 193 other people. This is one of the greatest makeovers ever, in his own words. He expanded on this metaphor in regards to the pandemic in 2020 by writing: "If we 7.5 billion people are now confined to a virus-infected cruise ship, does it make sense to clean and scrub only our own cabins while disregarding the hallways and air wells outside, via which the virus travels? No, is the obvious response. But that's exactly what we've been doing. Humanity must care for the entire world boat since we are all now in the same boat.

In an interdependent world, all hazards have a profound impact on one another thanks to a web of intricate interactions. In such circumstances, it is no longer true to say that an economic risk will just affect the economy or that an environmental risk won't have an impact on risks of a different sort (economic, geopolitical, etc.). We can all see political risks developing from economic ones (such as a dramatic increase in unemployment causing localized social upheaval), or societal risks developing from technology ones (such as the issue of tracing the pandemic on mobile phones provoking a societal backlash). Individual risks, whether economic, geopolitical, sociological, or environmental in nature, provide the misleading impression that they may be contained or reduced when seen in isolation; in actuality, systemic interconnection reveals this to be a constructed idea. Risks amplify one another in a world where everything is interdependent, which has cascading repercussions. Because of this, connection and closeness cannot be equated with isolation or containment.

This is evident in the chart that follows, which was taken from the World Economic Forum's Global Risks Report 2020. It demonstrates the interconnectedness of the dangers that affect us all as a group; each risk always overlaps with risks from its own macro category as well as threats from other macro categories (economic risks appear in blue, geopolitical in orange, societal in red, environmental in green and technological in purple). In this way, each risk carries the potential to trigger further hazards, potentially having a cascading effect. A "risk of infectious illnesses" is bound to have a direct impact on "failure of global governance," "social instability," "unemployment," "fiscal crises," and "involuntary migration," as the figure makes apparent (to name just a few). Each of these, in turn, will have an impact on further individual risks, such that the initial individual risk (in this case, "infectious diseases") ends up amplifying numerous more hazards, both within its own macro category (societal risks) and within the other four macro categories as well. This illustrates the systemic interconnectedness phenomena of contagion. We examine what the pandemic risk might entail from an economic, sociological, geopolitical, environmental, and technological standpoint in the following sub-chapters.

Interdependence invalidates "silo thinking," which has a significant conceptual impact. It is pointless and ineffective to solve a problem, evaluate an issue, or assess a danger in isolation from the others because conflation and systemic connection are what eventually matter. In the past, this "silo thinking" has been a contributing factor to why so few political scientists and economists correctly predicted the Arab Spring and the credit crisis, respectively (in 2011). The pandemic problem still exists today. Crossing disciplinary boundaries is challenging (and occasionally impossible) for epidemiologists, public-health experts, economists, social scientists, and all other scientists and professionals who work to help decision-makers grasp what lies ahead. Because of this, dealing with complex trade-offs, like controlling the spread of the virus versus reopening the economy, is incredibly challenging. It makes sense that the majority of experts eventually become specialized in ever-tinier areas. As a result, they lack the wider perspective required to join the numerous dots and create the more comprehensive picture that the decision-makers so sorely need.

Velocity

The aforementioned clearly identifies globalization and technological advancement as the main "culprits" for growing interdependence. A culture of immediacy has also been cultivated, and it is accurate to say that things move considerably more quickly now than they did in the past. The internet would surely be the item to point to in order to explain this astounding improvement in speed. In comparison to fewer than 8% twenty years ago, more than half (52%) of the world's population is now online, and in 2019, more than 1.5 billion cellphones - a sign and vector of velocity that enables us to be reached anywhere and at any time - were sold globally. In real time, 22 billion gadgets are currently connected by the internet of things (IoT), including electric grids, water station pumps, culinary ovens, and agricultural irrigation systems in addition to vehicles, hospital beds, and other objects. In 2030, this number is anticipated to be at least 50 billion. Other arguments for the increase in velocity also include the "scarcity" component: as civilizations become wealthier, time gains value and is viewed as being ever more precious. They have no time to waste, which may help to explain why wealthy cities always have quicker walking speeds than poor cities. Whatever the underlying cause, it is obvious that we are all experiencing constant, albeit discontinuous, rapid change in our roles as consumers and producers, partners and parents, leaders and followers.

Everything is moving quickly these days, including crises, social unrest, technology advancements and acceptance, geopolitical upheaval, the financial markets, and, of course, the appearance of contagious diseases. We live in a real-time society as a result, and we frequently feel as though life is moving at an increasingly rapid pace. In all facets of our life, from "just-in-time" supply chains to "high-frequency" trading, from speed dating to fast food, this new culture of immediacy and obsession with speed is evident. This new phenomena is so ubiquitous that some commentators refer to it as the "dictatorship of urgency." Indeed, it can manifest in dramatic ways. Scientists at Microsof have discovered, for instance, that a website can lose visitors to "faster" rivals by being slower by as little as 250 milliseconds (a quarter of a second)! The overall effect is a rapid and frequently unpredictable reduction in the shelf life of a policy, a product, an idea, and the life cycle of a decision-maker or a project.

Nothing more clearly shown this than how quickly COVID-19 advanced in March 2020. From the chaos caused by the unbelievable rapidity with which the pandemic seized the majority of the planet, a complete new age seemed to arise in less than a month. The outbreak was initially believed to have started in China at some point in the past, but due to our general cognitive difficulty understanding the significance of exponential growth, the exponential global spread of the pandemic caught many decision-makers and the majority of the public by surprise. In terms of "days for doubling," keep in mind that registered cases (or deaths) will double in just over two days if a pandemic spreads at a rate of 30% per day, as COVID-19 did in the middle of March for some of the nations that were most severely afflicted. It will take between four and five days if it develops at a rate of 20%, and slightly over a week if it grows at a rate of 10%. To put it another way, COVID-19 took three months to reach 100,000 instances globally, 12 days to double that number to 200,000 cases, 4 days to reach 300,000 cases, and then 400,000 and 500,000 cases.

Each case was completed in two days. These figures are tremendous velocity in action, and they make our brains spin! We frequently deal with exponential development by acquiring exponential "myopia," thinking of it as nothing more than "extremely fast," because it is so perplexing to our cognitive processes. Understanding this growth dynamic and the power of exponentials helps to explain why velocity is such a problem and why the speed of intervention to slow the rate of growth is so important. In a famous experiment conducted in 1975, two psychologists discovered that when we have to predict an exponential process, we frequently underestimate it by a factor of 10. This is what Ernest Hemingway recognized. Two characters in his book The Sun Also Rises converse as follows: "How did you go bankrupt? The same thing tends to happen for significant systemic shifts and disruption in general: things tend to change gradually at first and then all at once. Expect the same for the macro reset. "Two ways," Mike replied.

The effects of "impatience", for example, can be seen similarly in the behavior of participants in the financial markets (with new research suggesting that momentum trading, based on velocity, leads stock prices to deviate persistently from their fundamental value or "correct" price), as well as in that of voters in an election, the latter of which will have a critical relevance in the port

Velocity also caused many observers to establish a false equivalence by comparing seasonal flu with COVID-19; this comparison, made repeatedly in the early months of the pandemic, was misleading and conceptually incorrect. Let's use the example of the US to better illustrate the point and understand the role played by velocity in all of this.

The comparison ends there, however, and is meaningless for two reasons:

1) The flu numbers correspond to the estimated total flu burden while the COVID-19 figures are confirmed cases

2) The seasonal flu cascades in "gentle waves over a period of (up to six) months in an even pattern while the COVID-19 virus spreads like tsunami in a hotspot pattern (in a few cities and regions where I have personally observed it).

The first and second reasons are primarily due to speed: in the vast majority of countries, the epidemic's rapid spread made it impossible to have adequate testing capabilities, and it then overtaxed many national health systems that were designed to handle a predictable, recurrent, and relatively slow seasonal flu but not a "superfast" pandemic.

For politicians and business leaders, the need to gain a strategic perspective collides ever-more frequently with the daily pressures of immediate decisions, particularly obvious in the context of the pandemic, and reinforced by complexity, as we see in the next section. This is another significant and far-reaching consequence of velocity: decision-makers have more information and more analysis than ever before, but less time to decide.

Complexity

Complex systems are characterized by an absence of visible causal links between their elements, which makes them virtually impossible to predict. The behavior of a pandemic is influenced by factors such as the role of businesses, economic policies, government intervention, healthcare politics, or national governance. The COVID-19 pandemic has exposed this quantum world, which is highly interconnected and uncertain. Pandemics take advantage of trade routes and the tension that exists between public health and economics. The economic consequences can persist for as long as 40 years, depressing real rates of return.

As of June 2020, around half a year after the outbreak began, we still don't fully understand just how dangerous COVID-19 is. With the pandemic, it is generally known that a wide range of probable outcomes is possible, subject to unanticipated circumstances and random occurrences. Policy-makers need to be ready for another 18 to 24 months of pandemic activity. A full-fledged economic recovery cannot take place until the virus is eradicated. Governments must do whatever it takes and spend whatever it costs in the interests of our health and wealth.

The economic and societal damage of a lockdown is glaringly obvious to everybody, while success in terms of containing the outbreak and preventing deaths is more or less invisible. Some US data collected in early phases of reopening in some states showed a drop in spending and working even before the lockdown. Before March 2020, never had the world economy come to such an abrupt and brutal stop. With the pandemic, disaster-like macroeconomic outcomes happened in March 2020 over the course of just three weeks. The length and acuteness of the downturn, and its subsequent hit to growth and employment, depend on three things.

The US service sector was hit the hardest by the recent global pandemic. A full return to "normal" cannot be envisaged before a vaccine is available, writes Andrew Keen. Keen: The next hurdle is the political challenge of vaccinating enough people worldwide. The new reality of an 80 percent economy begs the question of whether possible shutdowns of business activity in the service sector will have lasting effects on the broader economy. Such a scenario will almost inevitably lead to a collapse in investment among business and a surge in precautionary saving among consumers.

It is too early to tell how GDP growth will evolve after economic lockdowns. The US personal savings rate increased to 33% in April (admittedly during the lockdown) while the eurozone household savings rate rose to 19%. Both rates will decline significantly as the economies reopen, but probably not enough to prevent these rates remaining at historically high levels.

Employment

Even the most experienced policy-makers are nearly speechless (and worse yet, nearly "policy-less") due to the devastation the pandemic is causing to the economy's labor market. In testimony before the US Senate Committee on Banking on 1 May, Federal Reserve System chairman Jerome "Jay" Powell admitted: "This precipitous decline in economic activity has caused a level of pain that is hard to capture in words.

In the US, a sign of problems to come elsewhere, it is predicted that the official rate of unemployment could peak at 25% in 2020, a level equivalent to that of the Great Depression, and that would be even higher if hidden unemployment were to be taken into account. The level of global unemployment will ultimately depend on the depth of the collapse in economic activity, but hovering around or exceeding two-digit levels across the world are a given.

Regarding GDP growth, each nation will be impacted differently depending on its economic structure and the nature of its social contract, but the US and Europe offer two radically different models of how the issue is being addressed by policy-makers and of what lies ahead.

In April 2020, the US unemployment rate had risen by 11.2 percentage points compared to February, while during the same period in Germany, it had increased by less than one percentage point. Two factors account for this striking difference: 1) the US labour market has a "hire-and-fire" culture that doesn't exist and is frequently practiced, while in Germany, it had increased by less than one percentage point.

In contrast to Europe, where governments decided to directly support those companies that kept workers formally "employed" in their original jobs, even when they were no longer working, the US government has so far (June 2020) provided income support for those who lost their job, with the occasional result that those displaced are better off than in their full-time jobs before the crisis.

Many other European countries came up with similar solutions, without which lay-offs and redundancies would have been much more detrimental. In Germany, the short-time working scheme (called Kurzarbeit - a model emulated elsewhere) replaced up to 60% of earnings for 10 million employees who would have otherwise lost their jobs, while in France a similar scheme also compensated a similar number of workers by providing them with up to 80% of their previous salary.

In many European countries, firms that can demonstrate that their liquidity issues were caused by the pandemic won't be required to file for bankruptcy until later (possibly as late as March 2021 in some countries). This makes eminent sense if the recovery takes hold, but it could be that this policy is only postponing the problem. Glow

This won't happen before a vaccine or a treatment is found, meaning that many people will be doubly worried - about losing their job and about not finding another one if they do lose it (which will lead to a sharp increase in savings rates). In a slightly more distant time (from a few mons to a few years), the unemployment situation is bound to deteriorate further because it cannot improve significantly until a sustainable economic recovery begins.

In the technology chapter, we analyze in more detail the impact that the pandemic is having on automation, but there is already ample evidence that it is accelerating the pace of transformation.

The COVID-19 crisis, and the accompanying measures of social alienation, have suddenly accelerated this process of innovation and technological change. Chatbots, which frequently use the same voice recognition technology behind Amazon's Alexa, and other software that can replace tasks typically performed by human employees were being gradually introduced to automate some of the tasks performed by human employees in the pre-pandemic era.

"Automation anxiety" is therefore set for a revival, which the economic recession will exacerbate. The process of automation is never linear; it tends to happen in waves and often in tough economic times, when the decline in companies' revenues makes labour costs relatively more exorbitant. For some time to come, consumers may prefer automated services to face-to-face interactions.

We know and understand that levels of unemployment are bound to rise globally in the foreseeable future, but over the coming years and decades we may be surprised. We could witness an unprecedented wave of innovation and creativity driven by new methods and tools of production. There might also be a global explosion of hundancies. It is easy to succumb to excessive pessimism because we human beings find it much easier to visualize what is disappearing than what is coming next.

Industries that will hopefully employ hundreds of millions of people. Of course, we cannot know what the future holds, except that much will depend on the trajectory of future economic growth.

What Future Growth Could Look Like.

According to current projections, the new economic "normal" in the post-pandemic era may be marked by much lower growth than in previous decades. As the recovery gets underway, quarter-to-quarter GDP growth may look impressive (because it will start from a very low basis), but it may take years before the overall size of most nations' economies returns to their pre-pandemic level.

With the economic emergency responses to the pandemic now in place, the opportunity can be seized to make the kind of institutional changes and policy decisions that will put economies on a new path towards a fairer, greener future. The history of radical rethinking in the years following World War II, which included the establishment of the Bretton Woods Institution for International Settlements, shows that societies have been forced to pause and reflect on what is truly of value.

This begs two questions: I what ought to be the new compass for measuring progress?

(ii) What will the new forces behind an inclusive and sustainable economy be?

Historically, national statistics were gathered primarily to give governments a better understanding of the available resources for taxation and waging war. As democracies grew stronger, in the 1930s the remit of national statistics was extended to capture the economic well-being of all citizens and the planet.

First, GDP must be updated to reflect the value created in the digital economy, the value created through unpaid work, as well as the value that may be destroyed through certain types of economic activity. The exclusion of value created through work carried out in the household has been a long-standing issue and research efforts to create a measurement framework will need new momentum.

With income inequality more pronounced than ever in many countries and technological advancements fueling further polarization, total GDP or averages such as GDP per capita are becoming less and less useful as true indicators of individuals' quality of life. Second, it is not only the overall size of the economy that matters but also the distribution of gains and the progressive evolution of access to opportunity.

Third, resilience will need to be better measured and monitored to gauge the true health of an economy, including the factors that determine productivity, including institutions, infrastructure, human capital, and innovation ecosystems, which are crucial for the overall strength of a system.

Although difficult to measure, natural and social capital are essential to the social cohesion and environmental sustainability of a nation and should not be undervalued. Recent academic efforts are beginning to tackle the measurement challenge by combining public- and private-sector data sources.

Real examples of a shift in policy-makers' emphasis are appearing. It is no coincidence that in 2019, a country placed in the top 10 ranking of the World Happiness Report unveiled a "well-being budget". The Prime Minster of New Zealand's decision to earmark money for social issues, such as mental health, child poverty and family violence, made well-being an explicit goal of public policy. In so doing, Prime Minister Ardern turned into policy what everybody has known for years that an increase in GDP does no guarantee an improvement in living standards and social welfare.

Additionally, several institutions and organizations, ranging from cities to the European Commission, are reflecting on options that would sustain future economic activity at a level that matches the satisfaction of our material needs with the respect of our planetary boundaries. The municipality of Amsterdam is the first in the world to have formally committed to this framework as a starting point for public policy decisions in the post-pandemic world. The framework resembles a "doughnut" in which the inner ring represents the minimum we need to lead a good life (as enunciated by the UN's Sustainable

Developmen Goals) and the outer ring the ecological ceiling defined by earth-system scientists (which highlights the boundaries not to be crossed by human activity to avoid environmentally negative impact on climate, soil, oceans, the ozone layer, freshwater and biodiversity). In between the two rings is the sweet spot (or "dough") where our human needs and those of the planet are being met.

We do not know yet whether the "tyranny of GDP growth" will come to an end, but different signals suggest that the pandemic may accelerate changes in many of our well-entrenched social norms. If we collectively recognize that, beyond a certain level of wealth defined by GDP per capita, happiness depends more on intangible factors such as accessible healthcare and a robust social fabric than on material consumption, then values as different as the respect for the environment, responsible eating, empathy or generosity may gain ground and progressively come to characterize the new social norms.

Beyond the immediate ongoing crisis, in recent years the role of economic growth in advancing living standards has varied depending on context. In high-income economies, productivity growth has been steadily declining since the 1970s, and it has been argued that there are currently no clear policy avenues for reviving long-term growth. In addition, the growth that did materialize disproportionately accrued to individuals at the top end of the income distribution. A more effective approach may be for policy-makers to target welfare-enhancing interventions more directly. In low- and middle-income countries, the benefits of economic growth have lifted millions out of poverty in large emerging markets. The policy options to boost growth performance are better known (e.g. addressing basic distortions), yet new approaches will have to be found as the manufacturing-led development model is fast losing its power with the advent of the Fourth Industrial Revolution.

The second important question about future growth is: What are likely to be the new drivers of this quality in the post-pandemic economy? Several areas have the potential to provide an environment that can foster a more inclusive and sustainable dynamism. If the direction and quality of economic growth matter as much as - or perhaps even more than - its speed.

The green economy spans a range of possibilities from greener energy to ecotourism to the circular economy. For example, shifting from the "take-make-dispose" approach to production and consumption to a model that is "restorative and regenerative by design" can preserve resources and minimize waste by using a product again when it reaches the end of its useful life, thus creating further value that can in turn generate economic benefits by contributing to innovation, job creation and, ultimately, growth. Companies and strategies that favour reparable products with longer lifespans (from phones and cars to fashion) that even offer free repairs (like Patagonia outdoor wear) and platforms for trading used products are all expanding fast.

Investment in childcare, elderly care, and other aspects of the care economy would result in the creation of 13 million jobs in the US alone and 21 million jobs in seven economies, and would result in a 2 percent increase in GDP growth in the countries studied. Education is another area of significant job creation, especially when considering primaries.

Governments therefore have tools at their disposal to shift towards more inclusive and sustainable prosperity, combining public-sector direction-setting and incentives with commercial innovation capacity through a fundamental rethinking of markets and their role in our economy.

As the critique of economic growth takes center stage, consumerism's financial and cultural dominance in public and private life will be overhauled. This is made clear in consumer-driven degrowth activism in some niche segments, like advocating for less meat or fewer flights.

However, beware of the pursuit of regrowth proving as directionless as the pursuit of growth! The most forward-looking countries and their governments will instead prioritize a more inclusive and sustainable approach to managing and measuring their economies, one that also drives job growth, improvements in living standards and safeguards the planet. The technology to do more with less already exists. There is no fundamental trade-off between economic, social and environmental factors if we adopt this more holistic and longer-term approach to defining progress and incentivizing investment in green and social frontier markets.

Fiscal and Monetary Policies

The fiscal and monetary policy response to the pandemic has been decisive, massive and swift.

In systemically important countries, central banks decided almost immediately after the beginning of the outbreak to cut interest rates while launching large quantitative-easing programmes, committing to print the money necessary to keep the costs of government borrowing low. The US Fed undertook to buy Treasury bonds and agency mortgage-backed securities, while the European Central Bank promised to buy any instrument that governments would issue (a move that succeeded in reducing the spread in borrowing costs between weaker and stronger eurozone members) (a move that succeeded in reducing the spread in borrowing costs between weaker and stronger eurozone members).

Concomitantly, most governments launched ambitious and unprecedented fiscal policy responses. Urgent and expansive measures were taken very early on during the crisis, with three specific aims:

1) Fight the pandemic with as much spending as required to bring it under control as rapidly as possible (through the production of tests, hospital capabilities, research in drugs and vaccines, etc.)

2) Provide emergency funds to households and firms on the verge of bankruptcy and disaster

3) Support aggregate demand so that the economy can operate as far as possible close to potential.

These measures will lead to very large fiscal deficits, with a likely increase in debt-to-GDP ratios of 30 percent of GDP in the rich economies. At the global level, the aggregate stimulus from government spending will likely exceed 20 percent of global GDP in 2020 with significant variation across countries, ranging from 33 percent in Germany to more than 12 percent in the US.

This expansion of fiscal capabilities has dramatically different implications depending on whether the country concerned is advanced or emerging. High-income countries have more fiscal space because a higher level of debt should prove sustainable and entail a viable level of welfare cost for future generations, for two reasons:

1) The commitment from central banks to purchase whatever amount of bonds it takes to maintain low interest rates

2) The confidence that interest rates are likely to remain low in the foreseeable future because uncertainty will continue hampering private investment and will justify high levels of precautionary savings. In contrast, the situation couldn't be starker in emerging and developing economies. Most of them don't have the fiscal space required to react to the pandemic shock; they are already suffering from major capital outflows and a fall in commodity prices, which means their exchange rate will be hammered if they decide to launch expansionary fiscal policies. In these circumstances, help in the form of grants and debt

relief, and possibly an outright moratorium, will not only be needed but will be critical.

These are unprecedented programmes for an unprecedented situation, something so new that the economist Carmen Reinhart has called it a "whatever-it-takes moment for large-scale, outside-the-box fiscal and monetary policies". Measures that would have seemed inconceivable prior to the pandemic may well become standard around the world as governments try to prevent the economic recession from turning into a catastrophic depression. Increasingly, there will be calls for government to act as a "payer of last resort" to prevent or stem the spate of mass layoffs and business destruction triggered by the pandemic.

The artificial barrier separating monetary and fiscal authorities from one another has been removed, making central bankers (to a relative extent) subservient to elected politicians. It is now conceivable that, in the future, government will attempt to use its influence over central banks to finance major public projects, such as an infrastructure or green investment program.

Politicians who have been elected will be subject to intense and constant public pressure to produce more and more "magic money tree," which is when the inflation problem arises.

Which Is Worse, Inflation or Deflation?

The decision to engage in perpetual quantitative easing (i.e., monetary finance) doesn't necessarily have to be made when the central bank purchases the debt issued by the government; it can be left to the contingent future to conceal or circumvent the idea that money "grows on trees." Second, the inflationary impact of helicopter money is unrelated to whether the deficit is large or small.

The deflation worry-makers point to a collapsing labor market and falling commodity prices, and wonder how inflation could possibly pick up anytime soon in these circumstances. The inflation worry-makers observe the significant increases in central bank balance sheets and fiscal deficits, and wonder how these will not, one day, lead to inflation, and possibly even possible deflation.

The combination of powerful, long-term, structural trends like ageing and technology (both are deflationary in nature) and an exceptionally high unemployment rate that will constrain wage increases for years puts strong downward pressure on inflation. At this point, it is difficult to imagine how inflation could pick up anytime soon. The reshoring of production activities could generate occasional pockets of inflation, but they are likely to remain limited.

Bond investors tend to think alike, but at the moment the low rate differential between nominal and inflation-indexed bonds paints a picture of ongoing very low inflation at best. Of course, this could change, but at the moment the low rate differential between nominal and inflation-indexed bonds paints a picture of ongoing very low inflation at best.

The possible "Japanification" of the (rich) world is frequently portrayed as a hopeless combination of no growth, no inflation, and insufferable debt levels. This is misleading. When the data is adjusted for demographics, Japan does better than most. Its GDP per capita is high and grows. High-income countries may well face a situation similar to that of Japan over the past few decades.

Japan's high living standards and well-being indicators offer a salutary lesson that there is hope in the face of economic hardship; there are peculiar reasons for this (a very high level of social capital and trust, but also labour productivity growth that surpasses the average, and a successful absorption of elderly workers into the labour force), but it shows that a shrinking population doesn't have to lead to economic oblivion.

What Will Happen To The USA Dollar?

The US has long benefited from the "exorbitant privilege" of holding the world's reserve currency, a position that has been "a perk of imperial might and an economic elixir". To a large extent, American power and prosperity have been built and reinforced by the international confidence in the dollar and the willingness of customers abroad to hold it, most frequently in the form of US government bonds (by managing sensibly its currency, like providing dollar liquidity to the global financial system efficiently and rapidly).

For quite some time, some analysts and policy-makers have been discussing a probable and progressive end to the dominance of the dollar. They now think that the pandemic might be the spark that proves them correct. Their reasoning is twofold and applies to both sides of the trust issue.

On the one hand (managing the economy sensibly), doubters of US dollar dominance point to the inevitable and sharp deterioration of the US fiscal position. In their mind, unsustainable levels of debt will eventually erode confidence in the US dollar. Just prior to the pandemic, US defence spending, plus interest on the federal debt, plus annual entitlement payments – Medicare, Medicaid and social security – represented 112 percent of federal tax receipts (versus 95 percent in 2017). This unsustainable path will worsen in the post-pandemic, post-bailout era. This argument suggests that something major will therefore have to change, either through a much reduced geopolitical role or higher taxation, or both, otherwise the rising deficit will reach a threshold beyond which non-US investors are unwilling to fund it. After all, the status of reserve currency cannot last longer than foreign confidence in the ability of the holder to honour its payments.

On the other hand (managing the US dollar sensibly for the rest of the world), doubters of the dollar's dominance point to the incompatibility of its status as a global reserve currency with rising economic nationalism at home. Even though the Fed and the US Treasury manage the dollar and its influentia network worldwide with efficacy, sceptics emphasize that the willingness of the US administration to weaponize the US dollar for geopolitical purposes (like punishing countries and companies that trade with Iran or North Korea) will inevitably incentivize dollar holders to look for alternatives.

Are there any viable alternatives? The US remains a formidable global financial hegemon (the role of the dollar in international financial transactions is far greater, albeit less visible, than in international trade), but it is also true than many countries would like to challenge the dollar's global dominance. In the short term, there are no alternatives. The Chinese renminbi (RMB) could be an option, but not until stric capital controls are eliminated and the RMB turns into a market-determined currency, which is unlikely to happen in the foreseeable future. The same goes for the euro; it could be an option, but not until doubts about a possible implosion of the eurozone dissipate for good, which again is an unlikely prospect in the next few years. As for a global virtual currency, there is none in sight yet, but there are attempts to launch national digital currencies that may eventually dethrone the US dollar supremacy. The most significant one took place in China at the end of April 2020 with a test of a national digital currency in four large cities. The country is years ahead of the rest of the world in developing a digital currency combined with powerful electronic payment platforms; this experiment clearly shows that there are monetary systems that are trying to become independent from US intermediaries while moving towards greater digitization.

Ultimately, the possible end of the US dollar's primacy will depend on what happens in the US. As Henry Paulson, a former US Treasury Secretary, says: "US dollar prominence begins at home (…). The United States must maintain an economy that inspires global credibility and confidence. Failure to do so will, over time, put the US dollar's position in peril". To a large extent, US global credibility also depends on geopolitics and the appeal of its social model. The "exorbitant privilege" is intricately intertwined with global power, the perception of the US as a reliable partner and its role in the working of multilateral institutions. "If that role were seen as less sure and that security guarantee as less iron clad, because the US was disengaging from global geopolitics in favour of more stand-alone, inward-looking policies, the security premium enjoyed by the US dollar could diminish," warns Barry Eichengreen and European Central Bank representatives.

Questions and doubts about the future status of the dollar as a global currency reserve are an apt reminder that economics does not exist in isolation. This reality is particularly harsh in over-indebted emerging and poor countries now unable to repay their debt often denominated in dollars. For them, this crisis will take on huge proportions and years to sort out, with considerable economic damage translating fast into social and humanitarian pain. In all these countries, the COVID crisis may well end the gradua process of convergence that was supposed to bring highly developed and emerging or developing countries into closer alignment. This will lead to an increase in societal and geopolitical risks – a stark reminder of the extent to which economic risks intersect with societal issues and geopolitics.

Resetting Society

Pandemics have historically strained societies to their very limits, and the COVID-19 crisis in 2020 won't be any different. Similar to the geopolitics we will witness in the following chapter and the economy we just saw, the societal upheaval caused by COVID-19 will linger for years, if not generations. The most obvious and immediate effect is that many governments will be criticized, with a lot of rage aimed at those politicians and policy-makers who have come across as unprepared or ineffective in their handling of COVID-19. "Nations cohere and grow on the notion that their institutions can predict tragedy, halt its consequences, and restore stability," wrote Henry Kissinger. Many nations' institutions will be seen as having failed once the COVID 19 pandemic is ended. This will be especially true for certain wealthy nations with advanced healthcare systems and significant investments in research, science, and innovation, where residents will wonder why their governments performed so poorly in comparison to others. As the "actual" offender, responsible for failing to ensure economic and social welfare for the majority of inhabitants, these may reveal the very core of their social structure and socioeconomic system. The epidemic will have a huge financial impact on less developed nations. It will make their existing social problems, including poverty, inequality, and corruption, worse. This might occasionally result in dramatic consequences that are as severe as social and societal disintegration ("social" refers to interactions between people or groups of people, while "societal" is the word that refers to society as a whole).

Are there any overarching lessons to be drawn from how the pandemic has been handled in terms of what has and hasn't worked? How much do various nations' responses indicate about the fundamental strengths and flaws of various civilizations or political systems? Some countries, including Singapore, South Korea, and Denmark (among others), appeared to be doing better than most. Others, like Italy, Spain, the US, or the UK, appeared to do worse than expected in a variety of areas, including crisis management, public relations, the number of confirmed cases and fatalities, and a number of other indicators. France and Germany, two neighbors with many structural parallels, had roughly the same number of confirmed cases as COVID-19, but a remarkably different number of deaths. What, outside variations in healthcare infrastructure, explains these apparent anomalies? As of now (June 2020), there are still a number of "unknowns" regarding the causes of COVID-19's particularly virulent outbreak and dissemination in some nations and regions but not in others. However, overall, the nations that perform better share the following significant similarities:

They were ready for what was about to happen (logistically and organizationally). They acted swiftly and with purpose.

They have a fair and affordable healthcare system.

They are high-trust societies where people have faith in both the government and the information it disseminates.

They appear to be under pressure to demonstrate a genuine feeling of togetherness, favoring the greater good over personal goals and interests.

The core societal values of inclusivity, solidarity, and trust are strong determining factors and significant contributors to the success in containing an epidemic, with the possible exception of the first and second attributes that are more technical (even though technicality has cultural elements embedded in it). Of course, it is far too early to predict with any degree of certainty what shape the societal reset will take in various nations, but some of its broad global features may already be identified. The post-pandemic age will, first and foremost, usher in a time of significant wealth redistribution, from the wealthy to the poor and from capital to labor. Second, COVID-19 is most likely to mark the end of neoliberalism, a body of principles and practices that favors competition over cooperation, innovation over regulation, and economic growth over social welfare. The neoliberal theory has been losing popularity for a while as more and more critics, business executives, and policymakers criticize its "market fetishism," but COVID-19 provided the final nail in the coffin. It is no accident that the two nations that have most fervently embraced neoliberal policies in recent years—the US and the UK—were also among those to see the greatest number of losses from the pandemic. Massive redistribution and abandoning neoliberal practices will have a significant impact on how our societies are organized, having an impact on everything from how inequality may lead to social unrest to the expanding role of governments and the redefining of social contracts.

Inequalities

One blatantly false cliche about coronaviruses is the idea that COVID-19 is a "great leveller."

The truth, however, is considerably different. Wherever and whenever it occurs, inequality has become worse as a result of COVID-19. As a result, it has no "leveling" effects in terms of medicine, business, society, or psychology. In actuality, the epidemic is a "huge unequalizer" that has widened gaps in opportunity, wealth, and income. It has made clear to everyone not only how many people around the world are economically and socially vulnerable, but also how severe and extensive their vulnerability is. This is a problem that is even more common in nations with weak or nonexistent social safety nets as well as weak family and social ties. Of course, this condition existed before the epidemic, but as we saw with other global concerns, the virus functioned as an amplifier, compelling us to face the seriousness of the issues with inequality that had previously been ignored by too many people for too long.

The initial impact of the epidemic has been to highlight the alarming differences in the level of danger that different socioeconomic classes are exposed to, hence amplifying the larger challenge of social inequality. During the lockdowns, a rough but telling story spread throughout most of the planet. The working class (for those with jobs) was not at home and was not in charge of their children's education, but was working on the front lines to help save lives (directly or not) and the economy – cleaning hospitals, working the checkouts, transporting people. The upper and middle classes were able to telework and self-school their children from their homes (primary or, when possible, secondary, more remote residences considered safer). In a highly developed service economy like the US, about one-third of all occupations can be done remotely or from home, with wide variations that are closely tied to sector-specific pay. While only 3% of the far lower paid workers in the food business can conduct their jobs remotely, more than 75% of American workers in banking and insurance can. Midway through the epidemic (mid-April), it became abundantly evident that COVID-19 was far from being the "great leveller" or "equalizer" that so many people had been alluding to at the start of the pandemic. This was especially true of the death toll.

Instead, it soon became apparent that the virus's method of spreading death wasn't impartial or fair.

In the US, African Americans, low-income individuals, and vulnerable communities, such as the homeless, have been disproportionately affected by COVID-19. Black persons made up to 40% of the deaths with COVID-19 problems in Michigan, a state where less than 15% of the population is black. The fact that black neighborhoods were disproportionately impacted by COVID-19 is merely a reflection of the inequalities that already exist. African Americans are less wealthy, more likely to be unemployed or underemployed, and suffer from subpar housing and living circumstances in America as well as many other countries. As a result, people are more likely to have pre-existing illnesses like diabetes, heart disease, or obesity, which makes COVID 19 more lethal.

The pandemic's second result was the exposure of the significant discrepancy between the fundamental nature and intrinsic value of a job well done and the financial reward it commands. Or, to put it another way, the people that society most needs are the ones we value least economically. The sobering reality is that the professionals who risked their own safety to care for the sick and maintain the economy during the immediate COVID-19 crisis are among the lowest paid in society. Examples include nurses, cleaners, and delivery drivers, employees of food factories, nursing homes, and warehouses. Their contribution to societal and economic welfare is frequently underappreciated. The occurrence is worldwide. But is especially pronounced in Anglo-Saxon nations where precariousness and poverty coexist. Not only are the people in this group the lowest paid, but they also face the greatest chance of losing their jobs. For instance, the vast majority (almost 60%) of community-based care providers in the UK work under "zero-hour contracts," meaning they are not promised a set number of hours or a fixed wage. Similar to this, temporary employment contracts with fewer rights than usual and no job security are frequently used for workers in food manufacturers. In Ken Loach's most recent film, "Sorry We Missed You," which vividly illustrates the dramatic extent to which these workers are always just one mishap away from physical, emotional, or economic ruin, with cascading effects made worse by stress and anxiety, delivery drivers are depicted as being paid per "drop" and receiving no sick or holiday pay.

Will social inequalities increase or lessen in the post-pandemic era? The inequities are probably going to get worse, at least in the near future, according to a lot of anecdotal data. As previously said, those with little or no incomes are being disproportionately affected by the pandemic because they are more likely to have immune deficiencies and chronic illnesses, which makes them more prone to contract COVID-19 and experience severe infections. In the months following the epidemic, this will continue. Not everyone will benefit equally from medical interventions and immunizations, much as with earlier pandemic periods like the plague. According to Nobel laureate Angus Deaton and Anne Case's co-authorship of Deaths of Despair and the Future of Capitalism, "drug-makers and hospitals will be more powerful and wealthy than ever," to the detriment of the poorest portions of the population. Additionally, by driving up asset prices, particularly in the financial markets and real estate, ultra-accommodative monetary policies implemented globally would widen wealth disparities.

Beyond the near future, though, the tendency might change and result in less inequality. How might that occur? The obvious inequity of the privileged treatment enjoyed only by the wealthy may have offended enough individuals to cause a significant societal backlash. In contrast to Europe, where underfunding of the healthcare system will no longer be politically acceptable, a majority or a very vociferous minority in the US may push for national or local authority over healthcare. It's also possible that the pandemic may eventually drive us to reevaluate the professions we genuinely value and revamp how we pay them as a society. Will society in the future tolerate that a prominent short-selling hedge fund manager, whose contribution to economic and social welfare is questionable at best, can make millions of dollars a year while a nurse, whose contribution to social welfare is undeniable, only makes a tiny fraction of that? In such a hopeful future, legislation would change to better both their working conditions and pay as we come to understand that many people in low-paying and precarious occupations play a crucial part in our communal well-being. Better pay would follow, even if it meant lower company profits or higher costs. Additionally, there would be intense political and social pressure to replace precarious employment and exploitative loopholes with permanent jobs and better education. Therefore, inequality might decrease, but if history is any indication, this hopeful future is unlikely to succeed without significant social unrest beforehand.

Social Unrest

Social instability is one of the gravest threats to the post-pandemic era. In some extreme circumstances, it might cause societal collapse and political collapse. Based on the evident finding that people frequently turn to violence when they are unemployed, have no source of money, or have no chances for a better life, countless studies, articles, and cautions have highlighted this particular risk. The problem's essence is best summed up in the following quotation. Although it applies to the US, its implications hold true for the majority of nations worldwide:

Others who are left without hope, employment, or assets may quickly turn against those who are in better financial standing. Approximately 30% of Americans currently have no wealth or negative wealth. If more people experience the current economic crisis without having access to health care, money, or jobs, and if they also feel angry and desperate, incidents like the recent prisoner escape in Italy or the looting that occurred there could occur.

Hurricane Katrina's aftermath in New Orleans in 2005 may come to be expected. Societies might start to fall apart if the government is forced to use paramilitary or military forces to put an end to, say, riots or attacks on property.

Social unrest had been rising worldwide well before the epidemic, therefore the risk is not new but has been exacerbated by COVID-19. There are many ways to define social unrest, but over the past two years, there have been more than 100 significant anti-government demonstrations worldwide [, in both wealthy and developing nations. These demonstrations range from the Yellow Vests riots in France to those against strongmen in nations like Bolivia, Iran, and Sudan. When governments ordered their populations into lockdowns in order to contain the pandemic, the majority (of the latter) were crushed by ruthless crackdowns, and many fell into sleep (like the world economy). It is difficult to think that old grudges and temporarily repressed social unrest won't surface anew, potentially with greater vigor, if the ban on gathering in groups and taking to the streets is lifted. There will be a significant increase in the number of hungry, sickly, anxious, miserable, and resentful people in the post-pandemic era. In diverse social groups, such as the unemployed, the destitute, the migrants, the convicts, the homeless, and all those left out, personal tragedies will accumulate and fuel anger, contempt, and impatience. Why wouldn't an eruption occur with all this pressure? Pandemics and social phenomena frequently share traits, and as was seen on earlier pages, both have tipping moments.

Disruptive social action is frequently a last recourse when poverty, a sense of being disenfranchised, and powerlessness reach a certain tipping point.

In the early stages of the crisis, well-known people shared these worries and warned of the rising danger of societal unrest. One of them is the Swedish businessman Jacob Wallenberg. He stated in March 2020 that if the crisis continues, unemployment might reach 20–30% and economies could decline by 20–30%. There won't be any healing. There will be dissatisfaction throughout society. Violence is inevitable. There will be severe unemployment as one of the socioeconomic effects. Residents will suffer greatly: some will pass away, while others will be miserable. With unemployment rates topping 20 percent to 30 percent in several nations around the world and most economies contracting in the second quarter of 2020 beyond what Wallenberg previously deemed to be concerning, we are already beyond what he deemed to be "worrying." What will happen next, where will social upheaval most likely emerge, and to what extent?

A worldwide wave of societal upheaval had already been sparked by COVID-19 as of the time this novel was being written. After George Floyd was killed at the end of May 2020, the Black Lives Matter movement began in the US, but it quickly expanded to other countries. COVID-19 was a key factor: George Floyd's passing ignited societal dissatisfaction, but the pandemic's underlying conditions—in particular, the racial inequalities it exposed and the rising unemployment rate—were the fuel that fueled the protests and kept them going. How? Nearly 100 African Americans have died in police custody over the past six years, yet it took the murder of George Floyd to spark a widespread revolt. The fact that this eruption of rage came amid the pandemic that has disproportionately afflicted the US African-American population is therefore not by chance (as pointed out earlier). By the end of June 2020, black Americans had a mortality rate caused by COVID-19 that was 2.4 times higher than that of white Americans. The corona crisis was also destroying black Americans' employment opportunities. This should not be shocking because there is such a wide economic and social gap between black and white Americans that black workers consistently outperform white workers on practically all measures. In May 2020, the unemployment rate for African Americans was 16.8% (compared to the national average of 13.3%), a highly high rate that contributes to a phenomenon sociologists refer to as "biographical availability": Lack of full-time job tends to raise the level of social movement engagement. We don't know how the Black Lives Matter movement will develop or what shape it will take if it endures. However, there are signs that it may be moving beyond racial discrimination. The demonstrations against systemic racism have sparked broader demands for economic justice and inclusivity. This makes sense as a transition to the inequality issues covered in the preceding sub-chapter, which also shows how risks interact and build upon one another.

It is crucial to stress that no circumstance is predetermined and that there are no "mechanical" causes of social unrest; rather, it is a reflection of a general human dynamic and frame of mind that depends on a wide range of variables. Outbursts of social discontent are classic non-linear occurrences that can be sparked by a wide range of political, economic, sociocultural, technical, and environmental causes, living up to the ideas of interconnectivity and complexity. They include diverse issues including racial tensions, food scarcity, and even feelings of injustice. They also include suffering brought on by major weather occurrences and economic shocks. Nearly invariably, all of these and more interact with one another and have cascade effects. As a result, while specific instances of unrest cannot be predicted, they can be anticipated. Which nations are most vulnerable? At first look, impoverished nations with inadequate social safety nets and wealthy nations with strong safety nets appear to be more vulnerable since they have fewer or no policy tools, such as unemployment benefits, to lessen the shock of losing income. Strongly individualistic civilizations like the US may thus be more vulnerable than those in Asia or Europe that either value solidarity more (as in southern Europe) or have better social systems for helping the less fortunate (like in northern Europe). The two can combine at times. Countries with robust social safety nets and strong senses of community include Italy (particularly in intergenerational terms). In a similar spirit, Confucianism, which is so pervasive in Asia, prioritizes community welfare over individual rights and sets a great priority on measures and norms that benefit the entire community. Of course, this does not imply that Asian or European nations are exempt from societal instability. Not at all! Even in nations with a strong social safety net but with low social expectations, violent and persistent forms of social unrest can develop, as the yellow vest movement in France showed.

However, it is important to emphasize that we are not helpless in the face of potential social unrest for the simple reason that governments, and to a lesser extent businesses and other organizations, can prepare to mitigate the risk by enacting the right policies. Social unrest negatively affects both economic and social welfare. Inequality is the main underlying factor contributing to societal instability. There are policy options available to combat intolerable levels of inequality, and governments frequently control these options.

The Reemergence of "Large" Government

According to Adrian Wooldridge and John Micklethwait, "The COVID-19 pandemic has made government important again. Not just powerful again (look at those once-dominant corporations pleading for aid), but also essential again: Whether your country has a solid healthcare system, skilled officials, and sound finances matters a great deal. The difference between living and dying is good government.

One of the most important lessons learned from the past five centuries in Europe and America is that severe crises help strengthen the state's authority. There is no reason why the COVID-19 pandemic should change what has always been the case. Historians point out that the need to wage wars, particularly those that occurred in far-off lands and necessitated marine capabilities, was always intimately related to the growing fiscal resources of capitalist countries from the 18th century onward. The Seven Years' War, which lasted from 1756 to 1763, is regarded as the first truly global conflict to involve all of the major European countries at the time. Since then, big crises have always been addressed by increasing the state's authority, beginning with taxes, which is "an inherent and necessary element of sovereignty belonging as a matter of right to every autonomous government." [66] A few examples that prove the point strongly imply that taxes will rise this time around just like they have in the past. The political and social justification for the increases will, as in the past, be based on the idea that there are "countries at war" (only this time against an invisible enemy).

The top income tax rate in France was zero in 1914; a year after World War I ended, it was fifty percent. In 1917, Canada implemented income tax as a "temporary" means of funding the war. During World War II, Canada drastically increased its income tax system by imposing a flat 20 percent surtax on all income tax paid by individuals other than businesses and by enacting high marginal tax rates (69 percent). After the war, rates decreased, although they nevertheless remained significantly higher than they had been. The same was true during World War II, when As the number of taxpayers increased from 7 million in 1940 to 42 million in 1945, taxation in America changed from being a "class tax" to a "mass tax." The two years with the highest tax rates in US history were 1944 and 1945, when incomes over $200,000 (about $2.4 million in 2009) were taxed at a rate of 94 percent. Such high rates would not fall below 80% for another 20 years, and were frequently criticized as confiscatory by those who had to pay them. After World War II, numerous other nations implemented analogous— and frequently draconian—tax policies. The top income tax rate in the UK increased to an astounding 99.25 percent during the war.

The ability of the state to levy taxes independently has occasionally resulted in observable social improvements in a variety of areas, such as the establishment of a welfare system. But these enormous shifts to something wholly "new" were always identified as a reaction to a violent outside shock or the expectation of one. For instance, most of Europe adopted cradle-to-grave state welfare programs as a result of World War II. Similar to the Cold War, governments in capitalist nations implemented a state-led approach to quell an internal communist uprising since they were so concerned about it. This system, in which state officials controlled significant portions of the economy, from energy to transportation, persisted far into the 1970s.

Today, the situation is fundamentally different because the state's role has significantly diminished in the Western world over the intervening decades. It is difficult to envision how an exogenous shock of the magnitude caused by COVID-19 could be managed with exclusively market-based solutions, hence this scenario is likely to change. The coronavirus was successful in shifting ideas about the intricate and delicate balance between the public and private spheres in favor of the latter almost immediately. It has shown that social insurance is effective and that shifting an increasing number of obligations (including those related to health and education) to people and the market may not be in society's best interests. In a sudden and unexpected turn of events, the notion that governments can advance the public good while unchecked, runaway economies can wreak havoc on social welfare may now become the norm, which was previously anathema. The needle has made a clear leftward shift on the dial that depicts the relationship between markets and government.

Governments now hold the upper hand for the first time since Margaret Thatcher epitomized an age by saying, "There is no such thing as society." Everything that happens in the post-pandemic period will force us to reconsider the role of governments. As argued by the economist Mariana Mazzucato, they should "advance towards actively influencing and building markets that generate sustainable and equitable growth" as opposed to merely repairing market failures as they occur. Additionally, they should make sure that public interest, not profit, is the driving force behind any commercial agreements that include government monies.

How will governments' newfound influence express itself? With the significantly enhanced and nearly immediate government control of the economy, a large portion of new, "bigger" government is already in existence. Public economic intervention has occurred very swiftly and on an unprecedented scale, as described in Chapter 1. Governments around the world announced stimulus programs totaling several trillion dollars in April 2020, just as the pandemic started to spread around the world. This was the equivalent of eight or nine Marshall Plans being implemented almost simultaneously to support the most vulnerable populations' basic needs, protect jobs whenever possible, and aid businesses in surviving. While governments began to increase social-welfare benefits, make direct cash transfers, cover wages, and suspend loan and mortgage payments, among other responses, central banks made the decision to lower rates and committed to providing all the liquidity required. Without governments, economic disaster and a total social collapse would have taken hold, as only they had the authority, capacity, and reach to make such choices.

In the future, governments will most certainly determine that it is in the best interest of society to change some of the game rules and permanently expand their involvement, albeit to varying degrees of intensity. A similar line of action is expected to prevail in the near future, just as it did in the 1930s in the US when extreme unemployment and economic insecurity were gradually handled by a stronger role for government. Let's quickly go over some of the most important elements before going over the form this will take in later sub-chapters (such the one after this one on the new social contract).

Either new health and unemployment insurance programs must be developed, or existing programs must be enhanced. In the Anglo-Saxon cultures that are the most "market-oriented," social safety nets will need to be expanded as well. To lessen the impact of the shock, prolonged unemployment benefits, sick leave, and many other social measures would need to be put in place. This approach will be aided by renewed trade union activity in many nations. Stakeholder capitalism will take precedence over shareholder value, which will now be a secondary factor. The financialization of the world, which has accelerated in recent years, is likely to reverse. Governments will be pushed to reevaluate many aspects of this fixation with finance, especially in the countries most impacted by it, the US and the UK. They could choose from a wide range of actions, such as outlawing share buybacks or forbidding banks from encouraging consumer debt. The public will scrutinize private companies more, especially (but not exclusively) for those that received public funding. Some nations will choose to nationalize, while others will favor taking equity stakes or making loans. In general, there will be more regulation covering many various areas, such as workers' safety or domestic sourcing for particular commodities. Additionally, businesses will be held accountable for the social and environmental problems for which they are expected to contribute to the solution. As an add-on, governments would vigorously encourage public-private partnerships so that private enterprises get more involved in the reduction of global hazards. Regardless of the specifics, the state's role will expand, having a significant impact on how business is done. Business executives across all sectors and nations will need to adjust to increased government involvement to varied degrees. We will vigorously pursue research and development for global public goods including solutions to the health crisis and the climate change. Because governments will need to improve their resilience capacities and want to invest more significantly in them, taxes will rise, especially for the wealthiest citizens. According to Joseph Stiglitz:

The first priority is to (...) increase funding for the public sector, particularly for those portions of it that are intended to guard against the numerous risks that a complex society faces, as well as to fund the scientific advancements and higher-quality education that are essential to our future prosperity. Researchers, teachers, and those who assist in running the institutions that support them can readily find work in these fields. Even as we come out of this crisis, we should be aware that there will undoubtedly be another crisis soon. The only thing we can be sure of is that it will look different from the previous one.

Nowhere will this governmental intrusion, which can take either a good or bad form depending on the nation and culture in which it occurs, manifest more forcefully than in the redefining of the social contract.

The Social Contract

The pandemic will likely lead many civilizations to reevaluate and revise the conditions of their social contract in various parts of the world. The fact that COVID-19 has acted as an amplifier of pre-existing conditions, bringing to the surface long-standing problems caused by profound structural frailties that had never been adequately addressed, has already been mentioned. A growing call to change the social contracts that more or less bind us all is expressing this contradiction and an emerging doubt about the current quo.

The (often tacit) set of agreements and expectations that regulate interactions between people and institutions is known as the "social contract" in its broadest sense. Simply put, it serves as the "glue" that holds communities together since without it, the social fabric will fall apart. Large portions of the population, especially those in the lower income brackets, have come to believe that the social contract is at best being eroded, if not in some cases completely breaking down, over the course of decades as it has slowly and almost imperceptibly evolved in a direction that has forced individuals to assume greater responsibility for their individual lives and economic outcomes. A useful and instructive illustration of how this degradation manifests in practice is the seeming illusion of low or no inflation. The rate of inflation has been declining for many years around the globe, but not for the three things that matter most to the vast majority of us: housing, healthcare, and education. Prices have increased significantly for all three, absorbing an increasing percentage of disposable incomes, and in certain nations, even putting households in debt to pay for medical care. Similar to the pre-pandemic period, employment opportunities had increased in many nations, but the rise in employment rates frequently occurred at the same time as wage stagnation and polarization in the workplace. Due to the fact that their income was no longer sufficient to support a fairly decent lifestyle, a significant majority of people's economic and social wellbeing eventually declined as a result of this scenario (including among the middle class in the rich world). Today, issues of inequality, the efficiency of most redistribution schemes, a feeling of exclusion and marginalization, and a general sense of unfairness are the main causes underlying the decline in faith in our social contracts. For this reason, a growing number of residents have started to express their outrage at a breach in the social compact and a general decline in faith in authorities. This widespread annoyance has manifested itself in some nations as peaceful or violent protests, while in others it has resulted in election victories for populist and extreme parties. Whatever its shape, the establishment's response has virtually always fallen short because it was unprepared for the uprising and had run out of ideas and policy options to solve the issue. Despite their complexity, policy solutions do exist, and they essentially revolve around modernizing the welfare state by giving people more agency and addressing calls for a more equitable social contract. Several international organizations and think tanks have adapted to this new reality over the past few years and have provided recommendations on how to make it happen. The pandemic will mark a tipping point by speeding this change. It has solidified the issue and rendered a return to the pre-pandemic status quo impossible.

What kind of structure may the new social contract have? Because each conceivable answer depends on the history and culture of the nation to which it applies, there are no pre-made, ready-to-use models. A "good" social contract for China will inevitably and understandably differ from one for the US, which in turn will differ from one for Sweden or Nigeria. The social and economic repercussions of the pandemic crisis have made their absolute necessity even more apparent, although they might all share some basic characteristics and ideas. Particularly, these two stick out:

1. The provision of social insurance, healthcare, and basic quality services is expanded, if not made universal.

2. Steps taken to improve protection for workers and those who are currently most vulnerable (like those employed in and fuelling the gig economy in which full-time employees are replaced by independent contractors and freelancers).

It is often claimed that a nation's response to a calamity speaks volumes about its strengths and dysfunctions, and first and foremost about the "quality" and robustness of its social contract. We should anticipate a great deal of soul-searching that will ultimately result in a rethinking of the conditions of our social compact as we gradually move away from the most intense moments of the crisis and start a thorough analysis of what went right and what didn't. In countries that were viewed as delivering a sub-par response to the pandemic, many individuals will start asking critical questions such as: Why is it that in the thick of the pandemic, my country often lacked masks, respirators and ventilators? Why wasn't it properly prepared? Does it have anything to do with our obsession with expediency? Why are we so inefficient at providing high-quality healthcare to everyone who needs it despite being so wealthy in terms of GDP? How is it possible that a person who spent more than ten years in medical school and whose year-end "results" are measured in lives gets paid meagerly in comparison to a trader or a hedge fund manager?

The COVID-19 crisis has made clear how insufficient most national health systems are, both in terms of the financial expenses and the personal consequences to patients, nurses, and medical personnel. Calls for more spending (and therefore higher taxes) will become louder in wealthy nations where tax-funded health services have long suffered from a lack of resources (the UK National Health Service being the most extreme example) due to political concerns about rising taxes. This is because people are beginning to realize that "efficient management" cannot make up for underinvestment.

The vast majority of welfare systems have glaring gaps, according to COVID-19. On the surface, the countries that behaved in the most inclusive manner are those with a complex welfare system, most notably the Scandinavian countries. To provide an example, as early as March 2020, Norway guaranteed 80 percent of self- employed workers' average salaries (based on the tax returns of the previous three years), whereas Denmark guaranteed 75 percent . On the other end of the spectrum, the most market-oriented economies struggled to keep up and displayed a lack of resolve in regards to how to safeguard the most vulnerable sectors of the labor market, particularly gig workers, independent contractors, on-call workers, and temporary employees whose employment entails income-generating activities that are outside the conventional employer-employee relationship.

Sick leave is a significant issue that could have a significant influence on the new social compact. Economists tend to agree that the absence of paid sick leave makes it harder to stop the spread of an epidemic, the basic reason being that if employees are denied access to it, they may be enticed or forced to go to work while they are infected and thereby transmit the disease. This is especially true for low-wage and service-sector employees (the two often go hand in hand). The American Public Health Association projected that during the 2009–2010 swine flu (H1N1) pandemic, 7 million people became infected and an additional 1,500 people passed away because contagious workers could not afford to stay home from work. Only the US has a system that allows employers to choose whether to offer paid sick time, out of the affluent economies. In 2019, roughly a quarter of all US workers (approximately 40 million, mostly concentrated in low-wage positions) did not profit from it. When the pandemic broke out in the US in March 2020, President Trump passed new legislation into law that temporarily mandated employers to provide two weeks of paid sick time and one week of unpaid family leave, but only for employees with childcare issues. It is unclear how this will be included into the US's revised social compact. By contrast, practically all European countries mandate employers to give paid sick leave for varied periods during which workers are also protected from dismissal. New legislation that were promulgated at the beginning of the epidemic also meant that the state would compensate part of or the whole wage of persons confined at home, including those working in the gig economy and freelancers. In Japan, all workers are entitled to up to 20 days of paid leave every year while, in China, they are entitled to sick pay that ranges from 60 percent to 100 percent of daily wages during any period of illness with the length of sick leave contractually agreed or defined between workers and employers. We should anticipate that these difficulties will become more and more intrusive as we redefine our social contract in the future.

Liberties and freedom are another factor that is essential for social contracts in Western democracies. There is rising concern that civilizations based on constant surveillance will emerge as a result of efforts to combat this epidemic and those in the future. A state of emergency may only be justified when a threat is public, universal, and existential. This topic is covered in more detail in the chapter on the technical reset. Political theorists also frequently stress that extraordinary powers must be circumscribed in scope and period as well as authorized by the people. The first element of the statement—"public, universal, and existential threat"—can be agreed upon, but what about the second? Expect it to play a significant role in future conversations about the ideals of our social contract.

Redefining the terms of our social contracts as a group is a monumental endeavor that connects the grave issues of the present with the aspirations of the future. According to Henry Kissinger, managing the crisis while securing the future is a historic challenge for leaders. Failure might ignite a global conflagration. We neglect the viewpoint of the younger generation who will be expected to live with it at our risk when we consider the structure we believe a future social contract might take. Their loyalty is unwavering, therefore we must remember to listen in order to better grasp what they desire. This is made even more important by the likelihood that the younger generation will be more radical in reshaping our social compact than the older one. Their lives have been completely turned upside down by the pandemic, and a generation will be marked by economic and frequently social insecurity as millions prepare to enter the workforce in the middle of a severe recession. They will endure these scars forever. Also, starting off in a deficit — many students having school debts – is likely to have long-term impacts. Already the millennials (at least in the Western world) are worse off than their parents in terms of earnings, assets and wealth. They are less likely to own a home or have children than their parents were. Now, another generation (Gen Z) is entering a system that it regards as failing and that will be afflicted by long-standing problems disclosed and aggravated through the pandemic. "Young people have a genuine desire for drastic change because we see the broken way ahead," a college junior who was quoted in The New York Times said.

What will the current generation do? By putting out radical answers (and frequently radical action) in an effort to stop the next catastrophe from occurring, whether it is social inequality or climate change. Due to its members' frustration and nagging conviction that the current system is irreparably broken, it will probably seek a major change from the current path of action.

Globally, youth activism is on the rise, and social media has changed it by enabling unprecedented levels of mobilization.

It can take many different forms, from non-institutionalized political participation to rallies and demonstrations, and it addresses a wide range of topics, including gender equality, economic reform, climate change, and LGBTQ rights. The younger generation is unquestionably leading social transformation. Without a doubt, it will serve as a catalyst for change and a crucial source of impetus for the Great Reset.

Reset of Geopolitics

Geopolitics and pandemics are linked in both directions. On the one hand, the chaotic demise of multilateralism, the absence of global governance, and the emergence of several nationalist movements make controlling the epidemic more challenging. The coronavirus is spreading throughout the world and harming everyone, while at the same time, geopolitical fault lines that separate countries encourage many leaders to concentrate on national remedies, which limits collective efficacy and hinders the ability to end the epidemic. On the other hand, it is obvious that the epidemic is escalating and speeding up geopolitical tendencies that were already perceptible prior to the crisis. What were they and how are geopolitical affairs currently?

There is no new global order; rather, the world is in a chaotic transition to uncertainty, as the late economist Jean-Pierre Lehmann (who taught at IMD in Lausanne) succinctly put it. Similar sentiments were recently expressed by former Australian Prime Minister and current President of the Asia Society Policy Institute Kevin Rudd, who was particularly concerned about the "coming post-COVID-19 anarchy" and said that various forms of rampant nationalism were replacing cooperation and order. Thus, the disorganized nature of the international and national reactions to the epidemic serves as a warning of what might occur on an even larger scale. The gradual rebalance from the West to the East, which creates tensions and, in the process, also leads to global disorder, has been years in the making and has many interconnected reasons. This is what determines geopolitical instability. The so-called Thucydides' trap, or structural stress, which unavoidably results when a rising power like China competes with a dominant power like the US, captures this. For years to come, the aftermath of this conflict will cause chaos, unrest, and uncertainty around the world. Whether one "likes" the US or not, its gradual withdrawal from the international stage (the equivalent of a "geopolitical taper," as the historian Niall Ferguson puts it) is certain to increase global unpredictability. More and more, nations that formerly relied on the US "hegemon" to deliver global public goods (for the protection of shipping lanes, the battle against international terrorism, etc.) will now have to take care of their own backyards. Country and influence will most likely be dispersed chaotically and, in some cases, unwillingly, in the 21st century because there won't be an absolute hegemon and no single power will achieve absolute domination.

With the partial and restricted exception of extreme Islam, conflicts and tensions in this chaotic new world characterized by a move towards multipolarity and the fight for influence will now be fueled by nationalism and the struggle for resources. Our globe will experience a "global order deficit" if no one power is able to keep the peace. We run the risk of entering a "age of entropy" in which retrenchment, fragmentation, rage, and parochialism will increasingly define our global landscape, making it less understandable and more disorderly, unless individual nations and international organizations are successful in finding solutions to better collaborate at the global level. This depressing situation has been made more obvious and worsened by the pandemic issue. No extreme possibility can now be ruled out due to the extent and effects of the shock it has caused. A split between China and the US that results in war, the implosion of certain failing states or petrostates, the potential dissolution of the EU, and many more scenarios are now feasible (though hopefully unlikely) ones.

The erosion of globalization, the lack of global governance, the escalating rivalry between the US and China, and the fate of fragile and failing states are the four major issues that will become more prevalent in the post-pandemic era and that intertwine with one another. We review these issues in the pages that follow.

Nationalism and Globalization

The term "globalization," which is used for a variety of purposes, refers to the international trade in products, services, labor, capital, and, as of recently, data. Although it has been credited for helping hundreds of millions of people escape poverty, it has been questioned for a while and has even started to wane. The globe today is more interconnected than it has ever been, as was previously mentioned, but for more than a decade, the economic and political drive that made the case for and promoted

Support for the expansion of globalization has been dwindling. The early 2000s saw the beginning of the first round of international trade negotiations, but no deal was reached, and at the same time, the political and social backlash against globalization was steadily growing. After the Great Financial Crisis that started in 2008, as the social costs resulting from the asymmetric impacts of globalization increased (especially in terms of manufacturing unemployment in high-income nations), the risks of financial globalization became increasingly clear. Thus coupled, they sparked the emergence of populist and right-wing parties throughout the world (most notably in the West), who, when in power, frequently turn to nationalism and push an isolationist agenda— ideas that are opposed to globalization.

The interconnectedness of the world economy makes it impossible to put an end to globalization. It can, however, be slowed down and even put into reverse. We believe the epidemic will accomplish it. It has already re-erected borders with a vengeance, strengthening to an extreme trends that were already in full view before it erupted with full force in March 2020 (when it became a truly global pandemic, sparing no country), such as stricter border controls (primarily due to concerns about immigration) and increased protectionism (mainly because of fears about globalization). In order to restrict the spread of the epidemic, tighter border controls are absolutely necessary. However, Dani Rodrik's "globalization trilemma" concept accurately recognized the risk that the resuscitation of the nation state may eventually result in far more nationalism. The Harvard economist highlighted why globalization would inevitably perish if nationalism increases in the early 2010s, when it was starting to become a contentious political and social problem. According to the trilemma, which is founded on the idea that only two things can successfully coexist at any particular time, the three ideas of economic globalization, political democracy, and the nation state are mutually irreconcilable. Only if globalization is restrained are democracy and national sovereignty compatible. On the other hand, if the nation state and globalization both expand, democracy will become unsustainable. Additionally, the nation state will have no place as globalization and democracy both advance. The trilemma's central paradox is that one can never choose more than two options out of three. The European Union is frequently cited as an example to highlight how relevant the trilemma's conceptual framework is. Combining democratic principles with economic integration (a stand-in for globalization) indicates that major decisions must be made at a supranational level, which in some way undermines the sovereignty of the nation state. The "political trilemma" paradigm contends that in the current climate, globalization must be restrained if we are to maintain some degree of national sovereignty or democracy. Thus, the growth of nationalism makes the retreat of globalization unavoidable throughout the majority of the world, with the West being severely affected. Two significant milestones of the Western backlash against globalization are the vote for Brexit and the election of President Trump on a protectionist platform. In addition to confirming Rodrik's trilemma, later research demonstrates that voters' opposition to globalization is logical in times of rapid economic growth and high inequality.

The global supply chain, which has come to represent globalization, will be the focal point of its "nuclear reactor" and the most obvious manifestation of increasing deglobalization. What will happen and why? Businesses who view it as a risk-mitigation mechanism against supply chain disruption (the resilience versus efficiency trade-off) and political pressure from both the right and left will both promote the shortening or relocalization of supply chains. In many nations (particularly in the West), the push for increased localization has been high on the political agenda since 2008, but it will now pick up speed in the post-pandemic era. Protectionists and national-security hawks on the right are the ones pushing back against globalization, and they were already mobilizing before the pandemic even began. They will now form coalitions and occasionally combine forces with other political groups that recognize the advantages of adopting an antiglobalization platform. Because of the good impact the epidemic had on our environment, activists and green parties on the left who were already demonizing air travel and calling for a reversal of globalization will feel more confident (far fewer carbon emissions, much less air and water pollution). Numerous governments will come to the realization that some trade dependency circumstances are no longer politically acceptable, even in the absence of pressure from the far right and green groups. How, for instance, can the US government tolerate that 97% of the antibiotics supplied to the nation are made in China?

In order to reverse globalization, supply chains will need to be shortened; this process won't be accomplished quickly.

Both incredibly difficult and expensive. For instance, a complete and total decoupling from China would necessitate investments of hundreds of billions of dollars in newly located factories from the companies making the move and equal sums from the governments to finance new infrastructure, such as airports, transportation links, and housing, to support the relocated supply chains. Although the political desire for decoupling may occasionally outweigh the practical capacity to do so, the trend's general direction is still obvious. This was made abundantly clear by the Japanese government, which allocated 243 billion of its 108 trillion yen rescue package to aid Japanese businesses in ceasing operations in China. The US government has made several allusions to taking such action.

Regionalization, an intermediary solution, represents the outcome that is most likely to occur along the globalization-no globalization continuum. The success of the European Union as a free trade zone and the recently proposed Regional Comprehensive Economic Partnership in Asia (a free trade agreement among the ten nations that make up ASEAN) serve as important examples of how regionalization may evolve into a new, more restrained form of globalization. Today, even the three countries that make up North America trade more with one another than they do with either China or Europe. As Parag Khanna notes, regionalism had already surpassed globalism before the epidemic revealed the flaws in our global interconnectedness. Globalization (as measured by the interchange of goods) had been trending toward becoming more intraregional than interregional for years, with the partial exception of direct commerce between the US and China. Early in the 1990s, North America took in 35% of East Asia's exports; currently, this percentage is down to 20%, primarily due to East Asia's share of its own exports, which is increasing annually as Asian nations progress up the value chain and consume more of what they produce. As a result of the trade war between the US and China in 2019, US commerce with Canada and Mexico increased while falling with China. At the same time, China's trade with ASEAN reached $300 billion for the first time. In other words, deglobalization was already taking place in the shape of increased regionalization.

As North America, Europe, and Asia place more emphasis on local self-sufficiency than on the lengthy and complex global supply chains that once embodied the spirit of globalization, COVID-19 will further hasten this global divergence. What shape may this take? It might reflect the series of circumstances that ended a previous era of globalization, but with a localized twist. Antiglobalization sentiment peaked in the years leading up to 1914 and 1918, then waned during the 1920s. However, the Great Depression sparked a new wave of antiglobalization sentiment in the 1930s, which led to an increase in tariff and non-tariff barriers that decimated numerous industries and caused significant harm to the world's largest economies. The same thing might transpire once more, with a strong urge to reshore spreading beyond healthcare and agriculture to encompass sizable categories of non-strategic goods. Both the far right and the far left will use the crisis to advance a protectionist agenda with greater restrictions on the free movement of people and capital. International corporations anticipate a return and escalation of protectionism in the US, not just on trade but also in cross-border mergers and acquisitions and government procurement, according to many surveys done in the first few months of 2020. What happens in the US will unavoidably have an impact elsewhere, as other developed economies erect additional trade and investment barriers despite advisories and pleas from international organizations to refrain from protectionism.

Although this gloomy picture is not unavoidable, we should anticipate that during the coming years, tensions between the forces of nationalism and openness will manifest themselves along three crucial dimensions: Global institutions, trade, and money flows are the first three. Recently, international organizations and global institutions have either been rendered ineffective, such as the World Trade Organization or the WHO, or they have not been up to the task, with the latter being more of a result of being "underfinanced and over-governed" than of inherent inadequacy.

As corporations shorten their supply chains and ensure that they are no longer dependent on a single country or business abroad for crucial parts and components, as we saw in the last chapter, global trade will almost likely decline. There may even be an ongoing process of de-integration in the case of highly sensitive businesses (like pharmaceuticals or healthcare materials) and sectors thought to be important for national security (like telecommunications or energy production). In the US, this is already a mandate, thus it would be remarkable if this mentality did not extend to other nations and industries. The so-called "weaponization of" geopolitics is also causing some economic harm.

Global corporations worry that they can no longer rely on the international rule of law to resolve trade disputes in an orderly and predictable manner.

International capital flows appear to already be under the control of national governments and public disobedience. Protectionist considerations will become more prevalent in the post-pandemic era, as numerous nations and regions have already demonstrated, including the EU, Australia, and India. To prevent foreign takeovers, national governments may invest in "strategic" companies or impose a variety of restrictions. Foreign direct investment (FDI) may also be subject to government approval. It is significant that the US government decided in April 2020 to forbid a publicly managed pension fund from making investments in China.

The rise of nationalism and increased international fragmentation appear to be driving some deglobalization in the upcoming years. While maintaining the status quo ex ante is pointless (hyper-globalization has lost all of its political and social capital and its defense is no longer politically viable), it is crucial to prevent a possible free fall that would cause significant economic harm and social suffering. A hasty withdrawal from globalization would lead to trade and currency wars, which would harm the economies of all nations, cause social unrest, and incite ethno- or clan nationalism. The only practical way to manage retreat is to establish a much more inclusive and equitable form of globalization that makes it sustainable, both socially and environmentally. Effective global governance and the policy solutions discussed in the final chapter are needed to achieve this. In the worldwide domains that have historically benefited from international cooperation, such as environmental agreements, public health, and tax havens, advancement is indeed conceivable.

The only way to do this is through stronger global governance, which is the most "natural" and efficient way to counteract protectionist tendencies. However, we are unsure of how its structure will change in the near future. The warning indications that it is not moving in the proper path at this time are alarming. Time is of the essence. The world will quickly become uncontrollable and extremely dangerous if we do not improve the efficiency and credibility of our international institutions. Without a worldwide strategic framework of governance, the recovery would not persist.

World Government

The UN asserts that "effective global governance can only be realized with effective international collaboration" since nation states enable global governance (one precedes the other). Pandemics, climate change, terrorism, and international trade are all global challenges that must all be addressed jointly in order to reduce their hazards. Even the most powerful nation states increasingly find themselves powerless to stop the major issues affecting humanity. As globalization, interdependence, and connectivity increase, global governance's ability to address them is gravely threatened by the return of nationalism. Global governance, in a nutshell, is the intersection of all these other problems.

Demonstrates the strong linkages between societal instability, national government failure, failure of global governance to address climate change, and the ability to effectively combat pandemics. It starts a vicious cycle in which nation states struggle to handle their most pressing problems. The pandemic demonstrated that the global governance structure was either nonexistent or dysfunctional. Nations ought to have united in a global "war" against the pandemic under an effective system of global governance. Instead, the attitude of "my nation first" took hold, greatly hampering efforts to stop the spread of the initial wave.

Bill Gates: "Now more than ever, the WHO is infinitely preferable to none at all". The WHO is not to blame for the failure of global governance, but only one of its symptoms. The UN agency lacks the authority to enforce pandemic preparedness or mandate information exchange. This dysfunctionality is a sign of a failing global governance system. If we do not fix global institutions, the world will become a very dangerous place.

After 40 years of strategic engagement, the US and China appear unable to cross the ideological and political gaps that separate them. Wang Huiyao, President of the Center for China and Globalization in Beijing, says the decoupling of the two countries' economies and technological advancements is "already irreversible". There is no "correct" or "wrong" view of world events, but there are divergent interpretations that are related to the place of origin, culture, and personal background of those who hold them. A "Chinese" view and a "US" view, along with numerous other views along that continuum, can coexist. When it comes to international events, the fact that two distinct witnesses are free to form their own opinions does not make those opinions any less genuine or legitimate.

There will be no winners, according to one set of people, while China has already won. The values and guiding concepts that have molded American public life since the nation's establishment heavily influence how the US sees the world and its place in it. Both China and the US are proud of their long histories (China's dates back 5,000 years), which causes them to overestimate their own advantages and underestimate those of the other. Kishore Mahbubani, a well-known observer of the conflict between the US and China, claims that China has taken over the role once played by the US, which was always the first to arrive with relief when it was required. He believes that the 6 billion people who make up "the rest of the world" are already preparing for the US-China geopolitical conflict.

Their decisions, which will be based on "the cold logic of reason," will determine who wins the rivalry match. The proponents of "US as a winner" argue that it is premature to call for an abrupt end to US supremacy in the post-pandemic era. The US government has significant geopolitical clout and can bar entire nations from participating in the dollar system. There may be a change in this, as we saw in the chapter before, but for the foreseeable future, the US dollar will continue to rule the world. The doubters of the "no winner" argument argue that China and the US are likely to emerge from this crisis severely diminished.

They contend that by emphasizing the achievements of tiny states, the crisis has revealed the shortcomings of superpowers like the US and China. The proponents of this theory contend that largeness involves diseconomies of scale. China might be attempting to take advantage of the situation by increasing its influence internationally. The US has faltered as a result of the pandemic crisis, and its influence has diminished. We know virtually little about how China and the US will compete strategically in the future.

It will veer between two extremes, from a gradual and manageable deterioration to a steadfast and complete enmity on the other. Africa is particularly susceptible to a COVID-19 pandemic because of the very nature of their fragility. According to estimates, there are currently between 1.8 and 2 billion people living in fragile states. The pandemic will be the exogenous shock that causes many of these regimes to collapse even deeper. Some of the most vulnerable communities in the world will be completely destroyed by the pandemic.

Millions of people rely on a meager daily wage to feed their families over huge portions of sub-Saharan Africa and some areas of Asia and Latin America. Any lockdown or health emergency brought on by the coronavirus could quickly spread despair and disorder. The decline of oil prices "only" implies a significant economic blow for Saudi Arabia and the Russian Federation. The impact might be disastrous for South Sudan, where oil relies for nearly all (99%) of exports. A wave of anti-government protests like to the Arab Spring in 2011 might be precipitated by the triple blow of COVID-19, the drop in oil prices (for some), and the freeze in tourism.

The World Bank predicts a 20% decrease in remittances to low- and middle-income countries, as a result of lockdowns and the subsequent economic "hibernation" that occurred in so many nations. This will cause a lot of hardship and make their economic, social, and political situation even more fragile. The UN secretary general's appeal for a global ceasefire on March 23, 2020, was ignored. At their peril, wealthy nations overlook the tragedy playing out in weak and failing nations. A new wave of mass migration in its direction will be one of the most evident knock-on effects for the richer regions of the world of economic hardship, unrest and hunger in the most unstable and poorest states.

How do pandemics, ecological collapse and climate change actually compare? They exhibit great differences while sharing many characteristics. The UN Special Envoy for Climate Action and Finance, Mark Carney, says climate change and pandemics are two very different diseases. He argues that a pandemic risk necessitates immediate action and will produce a rapid result. Climate change and nature loss occur gradually and cumulatively, with effects that are primarily visible over the course of the medium and long term.

SARS-CoV-2 induces COVID-19, making the connection between the virus and the disease in the context of the pandemic clear. It is significantly more challenging to directly link an environmental danger to a single incident. There is also a more fundamental reason: combating a pandemic does not necessitate a significant alteration to the underlying socio-economic structure and our spending patterns.

The Environment and The Coronavirus

Natural disasters and zoonotic diseases

Humans can contract zoonotic diseases from animals. The majority of scientists and environmentalists concur that they have sharply increased recently, especially as a result of deforestation (a phenomenon also associated with an increase in carbon dioxide emissions), which raises the danger of close contact and contamination between humans and animals. For a long time, scientists believed that the pathogens and viruses responsible for novel human diseases like dengue, Ebola, and HIV could only be discovered in natural settings like tropical forests and their diverse fauna. Today, we understand that this is incorrect since the causality is reversible. "We overrun tropical forests and other wild environments, which hold so many types of animals and plants - and among those organisms, so many unknown viruses," claims David Quammen, author of Spillover: Animal Infections and the Next Human Pandemic. We clear-cut woods, kill animals, cage them, and transport them to markets. Ecosystems are disturbed, and viruses are released from their natural hosts. They require a new host when that happens. Frequently, we are it. By this point, a growing number of experts have demonstrated that new viruses like COVID-19 are actually caused by people destroying biodiversity. These scientists have gathered around the emerging field of "planetary health," which investigates the nuanced and intricate relationships between human health, the health of other living things, and the health of entire ecosystems. Their research has demonstrated that the loss of biodiversity will result in an increase in pandemics.

100 animal and environmental organizations have wrote a petition to the US Congress estimating that the number of zoonotic diseases has doubled over the previous 50 years.

Land-use modifications have had the biggest relative detrimental effects on nature since 1970. (and in the process caused a quarter of man-made emissions). The economic activity that most disturbs nature is agriculture, which accounts for more than one-third of the earth's surface. According to a recent scholarly analysis, more than 50% of zoonotic illnesses have agricultural drivers. It is possible for infectious diseases to spread from animals to humans as a result of human activities like agriculture (along with many others like mining, logging, or tourism) encroaching on natural ecosystems. A wildlife disease reservoir is simply moved into a densely populated area when animals known to be associated with particular diseases (like bats and pangolins with the coronavirus) are removed from the wild and moved into cities, making the loss of animals' natural habitat and the wildlife trade particularly important. This may have occurred in the Wuhan market where the new coronavirus is thought to have first appeared (the Chinese authorities have since permanently banned wildlife trade and consumption). Most experts today concur that the likelihood of new epidemics increases with population growth, environmental disturbance, and increased farming intensity without sufficient biosecurity. Respecting and preserving the natural environment and actively protecting biodiversity are the most effective countermeasures we presently have to slow the spread of zoonotic diseases. It will be necessary for each of us to reconsider our relationship with nature and consider why we have grown to be so cut off from it if we are to accomplish this effectively. In the final chapter, we provide concrete suggestions for what a "nature-friendly" recovery might look like.

Air Pollution and Pandemic Risk

It's been known for years that air pollution, largely caused by emissions that also contribute to global warming, is a silent killer, linked to various health conditions, ranging from diabetes and cancer to cardiovascular and respiratory diseases. According to the WHO, 90% of the world's population breathes air that fails to meet its safety guidelines, causing the premature death of 7 million people each year and prompting the organization to qualify air pollution as a "public-health emergency".

We now know that air pollution worsens the impact of any particular coronavirus (not only the current SARS-CoV-2) on our health. As early as 2003, a study published in the midst of the SARS epidemi suggested that air pollution might explain the variation in the level of lethality, making it clear for the first time that the greater the level of air pollution, the greater the likelihood of death from the disease caused by a coronavirus. Since then, a growing body of research has shown how a lifetime of breathing dirtier air can make people more susceptible to the coronavirus. In the US, a recent medical paper concluded that those regions with more polluted air will experience higher risks of death from COVID-19 showing that US counties with higher pollution levels will suffer higher numbers of hospitalizations and numbers of deaths. A consensus has formed in the medical and public community that there is a synergistic effect between air pollution exposure and the possible occurrence of COVID-19, and a wors outcome when the virus does strike. The research, still embryonic but expanding fast, hasn't proved yet that a link of causation exists, but it unambiguously exposes a strong correlation between air pollution and the spread of the coronavirus and its severity. It seems that air pollution in general, and the concentration of particulate matter in particular, impair the airways – the lungs' first line of defence – meaning that people (irrespective of their age) who live in highly polluted cities will face a greater risk of catching COVID-19 and dying from it. This may explain why people in Lombardy (one of Europe's most pollute regions) who had contracted the virus were shown to be twice as likely to die from COVID-19 tha people almost anywhere else in Italy.

Lockdown and Carbon Emissions

The International Energy Agency (IEA) estimates in itsGlobal Energy Review 2020 that global carbon dioxide emissions will fall by 8% by 2020. This figure would correspond to the largest annual reduction on record, but it is still miniscule compared to the size of the problem. The biggest "offenders" in terms of carbon emissions aren't always those often perceived as the obvious culprits. If aggregated at scale, the pandemic could lead to a sustained reduction in carbon emissions. This brings us to the all-important question of whether it will have a positive or negative effect on climate change policies.

The pandemic is destined to dominate the policy landscape for years, with the serious risk that it could overshadow environmental concerns. Some countries could choose to pursue growth at "any cost" in order to cushion the impact on unemployment; others will focus on the environment when the pandemic recedes. COVID-19 made it clear that we ignore science and expertise at our peril, and that th consequences of our collective actions can be considerable. We have to recognise there will be other pandemics and be better prepared, but we must also recognise that climate change is a deeper and bigger threat that doesn't go away, and is just as urgent. These structural changes in how we work, consume and invest may take a little while before they become widespread enough to make a real difference but what matters is the direction and strength of the trend.

They see a need for distinct methods of non-violent action, including physical, virtual and hybrid actions. As we will see in Chapter 2, investors' activism will also be a force to be reckoned with. The European Green Deal is the most tangible manifestation yet of public authorities deciding not to let the COVID-19 crisis go to waste. The plan commits €1 trillion for lowering emissions and investing in the circular economy, with the aim of making the EU the first carbon-neutral continent by 2050. The World Economic Forum estimates that building the nature-positive economy could represent more than $10 trillion per year by 2030.

Climate change and its associated extreme weather events will be with us for the foreseeable future and beyond. Every measure destined to revive economic activity will have an impact on carbon emissions that will in turn have an environmental impact. A policy paper prepared by Systemiq in collaboration with the World Economic Forum estimates that building the nature-positive economy could represent more than $10 trillion per year by 2030 – in terms of new economic opportunities as well as avoided economic costs.

The WHO estimates that 90% of the world's population breathes air that does not adhere to its safety standards, which results in 7 million people dying prematurely each year. The effects of any particular coronavirus on our health are now known to be worsened by air pollution. People (regardless of age) who live in highly polluted cities will likely face a higher chance of contracting COVID-19 and dying from it. The International Energy Agency (IEA) predicts that the world's carbon dioxide emissions will decrease by 8% in its Global Energy Review 2020. According to a sustainability analysis, the total carbon emissions produced by the electricity needed to power and transport the data from our electronic gadgets is almost similar to that of the whole aircraft sector.

The Glasgow convention center, which was supposed to host the UN COP-26 Climate Summit in November 2020, was transformed into a hospital for patients in April. This brings us to the crucial question of whether the pandemic will ultimately have a beneficial or negative impact on policy related to climate change. All of these actions, if combined at scale, could result in a sustained decrease in carbon emissions. There are two possible outcomes for the fight against climate change in the post-pandemic age. First, governments may choose to "temporarily" set aside worries about global warming in order to concentrate on the economic recovery.

The second is driven by a new social conscience among significant portions of the general public that life can be different. Four in particular could succeed in creating a more sustainable and clean world. Four in particular could succeed in creating a more sustainable and clean world: The IEA's joint statement with Dan Jrgensen suggests that the shift to clean energy might help jump-start economies. Enlightened leaders will tie the terms of their stimulus plans to environmental pledges, they will, for instance, offer businesses with low-carbon business models more lenient financial terms. The epidemic served as a significant "risk-awakening," increasing our awareness of the dangers we all face and serving as a reminder of how interconnected our world is.

We reject science and knowledge at our risk and that there may be serious repercussions from our collective actions. During the lockdowns, we were forced to adopt "greener living," which resulted in a significant change in our purchasing patterns. This might persist, encouraging us to discard stuff we don't actually need and starting a positive feedback loop for the environment. For many of us, thinking about sustainability may seem like a luxury at this early stage of our difficult recovery. When things start to get better, we'll all remember that there is a causal relationship between air pollution and COVID-19.

It is impossible to foresee what the long-term repercussions of increased awareness and expertise may be, but it is certain that the power of the people has not decreased. Climate activists will step up their efforts and put more pressure on businesses and investors after seeing what they witnessed during the lockdowns (no air pollution). Investor activism will also be a force to be reckoned with. It pledges €1 trillion to make the EU the first carbon-neutral continent by 2050 (in terms of net emissions). Some cities, like Seoul, are strengthening their commitment to climate and environmental policy.

Many governments are beginning to take action to shift the system in favor of a new, environmentally friendly norm and convince the majority of people that this presents not only an urgent need but also a sizable opportunity. According to a policy document created by Systemiq and the World Economic Forum, creating a nature-positive economy by 2030 may provide more than $10 trillion annually in new economic opportunities and avoided costs. Every step taken to boost economic activity will immediately affect how we live, but it will also have an influence on carbon emissions, which will have an impact on the environment globally and over many generations. The threat from climate change, which is developing more gradually than the pandemic did, will nonetheless have very serious repercussions.

MICRO RESET (INDUSTRY AND BUSINESS)

At the micro level, that of industries and companies, the Great Reset will entail a long and complex series of changes and adaptation. For the majority of businesses stepping into the post-coronavirus future, the key issue will be to find the opposite balance between what functioned before and what is needed now to prosper in the new normal. In the post-COVID-19 era, apart from those few sectors in which companies will benefit on average from strong tailwinds, the journey will be challenging and sometimes treacherous. For some, like entertainment, travel or hospitality, a return to a pre-pandemic environment is unimaginable in the foreseeable future (and maybe never in some cases…). For others, namely manufacturing or food, it is more about finding ways to adjust to the shock and capitalize on some new trends (like digital) to thrive in the Post-Pandemic era.

We are in the early days of the post-pandemic era, but there are already powerful new or accelerating trends at work. For some industries, these will prove a boon, for others a major challenge. The macro reset discussed in Chapter 1 will translate into a myriad of micro consequences at the industry and company level. As a direct consequence of the pandemic, businesses that were already operating online are bound to benefit from a lasting competitive advantage. As more and diverse things and services are brought to us via our mobiles and computers, companies in sectors as disparate as e-commerce, contactless operations, robots and drone deliveries will thrive.s

It is not by accident that Alibaba, Amazon, Netflix or Zoom emerged as "winners" from the lockdowns. During the peak of the pandemic, O2O – online to offline – gained major traction. The phenomenon of blurring the distinction between online and offline has emerged as one of the most potent trends of the post-COVID-19 era. Io T offers companies the means to execute and uphold social-distancing rules, but also to reduce costs and implement more agile operations. Equipment maintenance, management inventory, supplier relations or safety strategies: all of these different activities can now be performed (to a large extent) via a computer.

Telemedicine, in particular, will benefit from the pandemic. It will accelerate the trend towards more wearable and at-home diagnostics, like smart toilets capable of tracking health data and performing health analyses. In Asia, the shift to online education has been particularly notable, with a sharp increase in students' digital enrolments. As the habit of shopping online becomes more prevalent, it will depress bricks-and-mortar retail still further. In the post-pandemic era, it is "end-to-end value optimization", an idea that includes both resilience and efficiency alongside cost that will prevail.

The pandemic has placed the last nail in the coffin of the principle that companies should optimize supply chains based on individual component costs. The advent of international production into ever-more intricate bits and pieces has resulted in a system run on a just-in-time basis that has proven to be extremely lean and efficient, but also exceedingly complex. Simplification is therefore the antidote, which should in turn generate more resilience. This means that the "global value chains" that represent roughly three-quarters of all global trade will inevitably decline. As a result, companies dependent upon them can no longer take it for granted that tariff commitments enshrined by the World Trade Organization will protect them from a sudden surge in protectionism.

In the post-pandemic era, business will be subject to much greater government interference than in the past. This includes conditional bailouts, public procurement and labour market regulations. In the coming months and years, a "regime change" might occur when policy-makers take on a substantial portion of private-sector default risk. The post-pandemic era will be a time of greater government interference in public policy and corporate planning. The scramble for ventilators during the peak of the pandemic epitomizes why.

It is unlikely that this sort of situation will reoccur in the post-patriotic era, as public authorities will think twice about outsourcing projects that have critical public-health implications. In the post-pandemic era, companies will have to pay higher taxes and various forms of government funding (like social care) the gig economy will feel the impact of such a policy more than any other sector. As the pandemic will radically alter social and political attitudes towards gig workers, governments will force those companies that employ them to offer proper contracts with benefits such as social insurance and health coverage. But others, such as consumer behaviour, the future of work and mobility, and supply-chain responsibility, will move to the forefront of the investment process and will become an integral component of due diligence. The conviction that ESG strategies benefited from the pandemic and are most likely to benefit further is corroborated by various surveys and reports.

Early data shows that the sustainability sector outperformed conventional funds during the first quarter of 2020. The debate between those who believe that stakeholder capitalism will be sacrificed on the altar of the recovery and those who argue that it is now time to "build back better" is far from resolved. ESG strategies and their future role in the post-pandemic era activism will make a difference by reinforcing the trend. For every Michael O'Leary (the CEO of Ryanair) who thinks that COVID-19 will put ESG considerations "on t back burner", there is a Brian Chesky (CEO of Airbnb) who is committed to transforming his business into a "stakeholder company". In May 2020, just as the epicentre of the pandemic was moving from the US to Latin America, Googl employees, emboldened by a report published by Greenpeace, won the company to no longer build custom AI and machine learning algorithms for upstream extraction in the oil and gas industry.

CONCLUSION

In Gabriel Garcia Marquez's Chronicle of a Death Foretold, an entire village foresees a looming catastrophe, and yet none of the villagers seem able or willing to act to prevent it. To avoid such a fate, without delay we need to set in motion the Great Reset. Failing to address and fix the deep-rooted ills of our societies and economies could heighten the risk that a reset will be imposed by violent shocks like conflicts and even revolutions. The Great Reset is about making the world less divisive, less polluting, less destructive, more inclusive, more equitable and fairer than we left it in the pre-pandemic era. Some may resist the necessity to engage in it, fearful of the magnitude of the task and hopeful that the situation will get back to "normal".

The argument for passivity goes like this: we have been through similar shocks – pandemics, harsh recessions, geopolitical divides and social tensions – before and we will get through them again. To do nothing is not a viable option. The death of George Floyd (an African American killed by a police officer in May 2020) was the first domino or the last straw that marked a momentous tipping point at which an accumulated and profound sentiment of unfairness felt by the US African-American community exploded into massive protests. What matters to African Americans is their situation today, not how much their condition has "improved" compared to 150 years ago. In all likelihood, unless the pandemic evolves in an unforeseen way, the consequences of

COVID-19 in terms of health and mortality will be mild compared to previous pandemics.

Much of what's coming is unknown, but we can be sure of the following: in the post- pandemic world, questions of fairness will come to the fore, ranging from stagnating real incomes to the redefinition of our social contracts. There is a real risk that tomorrow the world will be even more divided, nationalistic and prone to conflicts than it is today. But an alternative scenario is possible, one in which collective action within communities and greater collaboration between nations enable a more rapid and peaceful exit from the corona crisis. Nobel Prize laureate of the Nobel Prize in Economics Amartya Sen: "Can a better society emerge from the lockdowns?" Jared Diamond: The corona crisis will compel us to address four existential risks that we collectively face:

1) Nuclear threats

2) Climate change

3) The unsustainable use of essential resources

4) The consequences of the enormous differences in standards of living between the world's peoples.

 Among the pandemic's consequences, it could prove to be the biggest, the most lasting – and our great cause for hope. If the virus does at last prepare us to deal with those existential threats, there may be a silver lining to the virus's black cloud.

Thanks for Reading.

www.ingramcontent.com/pod-product-compliance
Lightning Source LLC
Chambersburg PA
CBHW071238170526
45165CB00003B/1142